Build Your Own Green PC

Other books in the Save a Bundle Series

Build Your Own Pentium™ Processor by *Aubrey Pilgrim*

Build Your Own Multimedia PC by *Aubrey Pilgrim*

Upgrade or Repair Your PC and Save a Bundle—3rd Edition by *Aubrey Pilgrim*

Build Your Own Low-Cost PostScript® Printer and Save a Bundle—2nd Edition by *Horace W. LaBadie, Jr.*

Build Your Own 80386 IBM Compatible and Save a Bundle by *Aubrey Pilgrim*

Build Your Own 80486 PC and Save a Bundle by *Aubrey Pilgrim*

Build Your Own Macintosh and Save a Bundle by *Bob Brant*

Build Your Own IBM Compatible and Save a Bundle—2nd Edition by *Aubrey Pilgrim*

Build Your Own 386/386SX Compatible and Save a Bundle—2nd Edition by *Aubrey Pilgrim*

Build Your Own Computer Accessories and Save a Bundle by *Bonnie J. Hargrave* and *Ted Dunning*

Build Your Own Macintosh® and Save a Bundle—2nd Edition by *Bob Brant*

Build Your Own Low-Cost PC and Save a Bundle by *Aubrey Pilgrim*

Build Your Own LAN and Save a Bundle by *Aubrey Pilgrim*

Build Your Own 486/486SX and Save a Bundle—2nd Edition by *Aubrey Pilgrim*

Build Your Own Green PC

Wallace Wang

Artwork by Rick Wilkins

Windcrest°/McGraw-Hill

New York San Francisco Washington, D.C. Auckland Bogotá
Caracas Lisbon London Madrid Mexico City Milan
Montreal New Delhi San Juan Singapore
Sydney Tokyo Toronto

Printed by Webcom Ltd., on 100% recycled and recyclable paper containing 75% postconsumer waste. The paper exceeds both Canadian ECP (Environmental Choice Program) and American EPA (Environmental Protection Agency) standards for recycled fiber content. The ink is water and vegetable-based, and the printing process uses nonheat-set presses, which release less volatile organic compounds into the atmosphere than conventional printing presses.

pbk 1 2 3 4 5 6 7 8 9 WEB/WEB 9 8 7 6 5 4

Library of Congress Cataloging-in-Publication Data

Wang, Wally.
    Build your own green PC / Wallace Wang.
       p.   cm.
    Includes index.
    ISBN 0-07-068156-2 (paper)
    1. Microcomputers—Design and construction—Amateurs' manuals.
    2. Microcomputers—Environmental aspects—Amateurs' manuals.
    I. Title
TK9969.W36   1994
621.39'16—dc20
                                           94-7918
                                           CIP

Acquisitions editor: Brad Schepp
Editorial team: Robert E. Ostrander, Executive Editor
                 Aaron G. Bittner, Book Editor
Production team: Katherine G. Brown, Director
                    Olive A. Harmon, Coding
                    Susan E. Hansford, Coding
                    Jan Fisher, Layout
                    Sandra Fisher, Proofreading
                    Jodi L. Tyler, Indexer
Design team: Jaclyn J. Boone, Designer
              Brian Allison, Associate Designer
Cover design: Richard Adelson, New York, NY
Cover photo: Kitagawa/Superstock, Inc.
Cover copywriter: Cathy Mentzer
                                          EL1
                                        0681562

Printed in Canada

Dedication
To my parents (Herbert and Ruth Wang), my wife (Cassandra),
and my cat (Bo).

Contents

Acknowledgments

Thanks go to my agents, Matt Wagner and Bill Gladstone at Waterside Productions, for their help and support in getting this book project off the ground. Additional thanks goes to Pete Balistreri for his invaluable assistance in putting this book together, Barry Diamond for always making me laugh at The Comedy Store no matter how many times I see his act, Dan Fitzsimmons for his invaluable assistance in putting the "green" PC together, and Jack Dunning for giving me my start in the wacky world of computer instruction and book publishing.

Introduction

Believe it or not, the personal computer may be one of the most environmentally destructive inventions of all time. Unlike cars, which clog our highways and emit poisonous carbon monoxide gases into the air; or aerosol spray cans, which release ozone-destroying fluorocarbons into the atmosphere; or pesticides, which indiscriminately kill both nuisance and beneficial insects as well as poisoning the water supply for plants, animals, and people alike; the destructive capability of the personal computer seems limited or even negligible at first.

But the truth is that the personal computer is more hazardous than many other inventions precisely because its destructive effects are so hard to identify. Just the process of making microprocessors alone involves a host of toxic chemicals like trichloroethylene (a known carcinogen), glycol ether (a known reproductive toxin), and chlorofluorocarbons (an ozone-depleting gas). Not only do these chemicals leak into the environment, but they also endanger the lives of chip manufacturing workers every day. Silicon Valley, long the cradle of high-technology firms like Hewlett-Packard, Fairchild Semiconductors, and IBM, has one of the highest concentrations of toxic waste contamination in the country. A study by the California Regional Water Quality Control Board discovered that 85% of all underground hazardous waste storage tanks in Silicon Valley had leaks, contaminating over 200 drinking water supplies around the county.

Even fully-assembled computers are not free from blame. The average computer comes packaged in several layers of cardboard and Styrofoam packaging, made from virgin paper stock that contributes to deforestation. The cardboard is often bleached white with chlorine, which is a major cause of pollution during the paper-making process. Advertisements, manufacturer's logos, and handling instructions are almost always printed on the cardboard using petroleum-based inks.

But the worst culprit is the computer itself. According to the Environmental Protection Agency (EPA), personal computers and related peripherals consume as much as 5% of all commercial electricity. By the year 2000, that figure will be closer to 10% and rising.

Besides the tremendous cost to pay for all this additional electricity to support this growing number of personal computers, each kilowatt of power generated requires the burning of natural resources like coal, oil, or natural gas. This in turn contributes to the release of carbon dioxide into the atmosphere (which causes global warming), sulfur dioxide (the chief cause of acid rain), and nitrogen oxide (smog).

Not only can a personal computer indirectly affect the environment, but it can also directly affect your own health as well. Poorly designed keyboards and computer desks may be directly responsible for affecting thousands of people with carpal tunnel syndrome, which is a disorder of nerves caused by the unnatural repetitive motion of the hands and wrists. According to the Occupational Safety and Health Administration, carpal tunnel syndrome accounts for over half of all work-related injuries.

Even your computer monitor may be more hazardous than you might think. Besides causing possible eyestrain and headaches from staring at a flickering, grainy screen all day, computer monitors are also responsible for extremely low-frequency (ELF) radiation and radio-frequency interference (RFI) emissions, suspected of causing leukemia, cataracts, miscarriages, breast cancer, and birth defects. Although there has yet to be conclusive evidence linking electromagnetic emissions to health problems, nearly everyone agrees that the less exposure the better.

So with computers fouling the environment, wasting electricity, and wrecking your health, you may be tempted to toss your computer out the window and go back to learning the slide rule and the abacus.

But there's another alternative.

Rather than eliminate computers altogether, there's a movement sponsored by the EPA to promote "green" PCs. This movement, dubbed the Energy Star program, encourages manufacturers to develop computers that consume up to 60% less electricity than their ordinary counterparts. Any computer that meets this requirement qualifies to use the Energy Star logo in their advertising and marketing campaigns.

Already several manufacturers, including Apple, IBM, AST Research, Gateway, Austin, Zeos, and Compaq, have released Energy Star-compliant computers. Eventually, every available computer and peripheral will meet the energy-conserving criteria defined by the Energy Star program, which requires that equipment consume less than 30 watts of power when not in use.

According to the EPA, the average Energy Star computer can save between $40 to $162 a year on electricity costs alone. As the world's largest buyer of computer equipment, the U.S. Government has taken the lead and will only purchase Energy Star computer equipment. The EPA estimates that this change alone will save taxpayers $40 million each year in electricity costs, essentially paying for the cost of the Energy Star program several times over. In fact, the EPA estimates that the amount of electricity saved by Energy Star computers could be great enough to supply Maine, New Hampshire, and Vermont with electricity each year. Thus the Energy Star program may become the most cost-effective government program in history.

Saving energy will definitely help conserve our resources and eliminate needless waste, but energy reduction alone may not be enough. All Energy Star computers may conserve electricity, but what about the hidden dangers of electromagnetic radiation, repetitive motion injuries, and wasteful packaging as well?

If you really want to save the environment and protect our resources, take responsibility for your computer and build your own "green" PC. By building your own computer, you can ensure that your computer only uses parts and equipment that meet at least one of the following four criteria:

- Conserves electricity along the EPA's Energy Star guidelines.
- Reduces or eliminates health hazards like electromagnetic radiation and repetitive motion injuries.
- Built or packaged using recycled plastics, soy inks, unbleached paper, and other environment saving materials.
- Built or sold by companies actively involved in recycling in-house or donating to environmental causes.

Not only will building your own computer ensure that your PC will be as "green" as possible, but you'll likely save money plus gain valuable knowledge and experience about fixing and upgrading your computer as well.

Whether you just want a "green" PC that meets the EPA Energy Star guidelines, or a super "green" PC complete with energy-saving peripherals, recycled toner cartridges, and low-emission monitors, this book can help you build a computer that meets your personal standard of "green."

Building your own computer is not hard, and this book will show you where to find parts, how to put them together, and how to judge different items for their impact on the environment. But above all, this book will show how you how to design, build, and use the highest quality, environmentally-friendly equipment possible, all without costing you any more than a "normal" PC.

Welcome to the future. "Green" computing is here to stay.

1
Getting started

If you can use a screwdriver, you can build a computer, and this book will show you how.

In the old days, building your own computer was about as inviting as building your own transmission. Unless you had the knowledge of an electrical engineer, the skill of an electronics technician, and the patience of a computer programmer, building your own computer was an impossible fantasy that only rocket scientists could indulge.

But not any more. Today, computers are built out of prefabricated parts that snap or screw together. Because so many companies make parts for computers, you have a wide variety of prices, features, and quality levels to choose from. These components make a basic system:

- A computer case
- A power supply
- A motherboard
- Memory chips
- A monitor
- A video card
- A keyboard
- A mouse
- One or more floppy disk drives
- A hard disk
- A floppy/hard drive controller card

The computer case holds everything together. The motherboard holds the central processing unit (CPU), the memory chips, the power supply, the video card, and the floppy/hard drive controller card. The floppy drive, hard drive, monitor, keyboard, and mouse either plug directly into the motherboard or into a card already plugged into the motherboard. Once you have these parts plugged in and working, you have a basic IBM-compatible computer.

Of course, who wants an ordinary, run of the mill, humdrum computer when you can have a supercharged, heavy-duty, powerhouse machine that can blow the doors

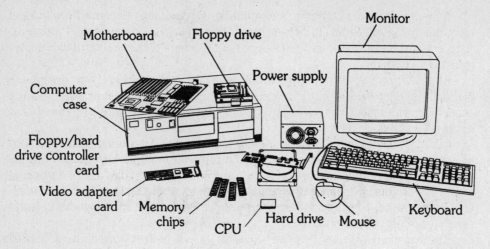

1-1 The parts of a computer.

off the best computer that IBM, Compaq, or Dell can put on the market? If that's more like your line of thinking, then you'll want to add optional equipment such as:

- A modem
- A printer
- A CD-ROM drive
- A scanner
- A sound card and speakers
- A tape backup drive

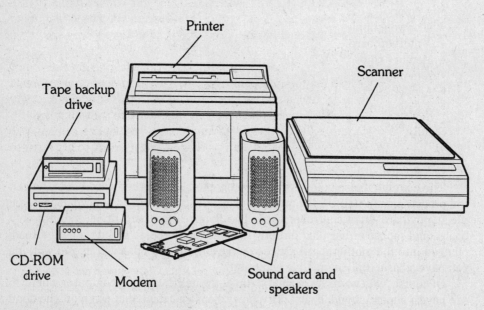

1-2 The optional parts of a computer.

A modem lets your computer communicate through the telephone lines to local electronic bulletin boards (BBSs), on-line services such as CompuServe, Prodigy, or America On-Line, or to computer users on the other side of the world through the Internet network.

Almost everyone needs a printer, but not all printers are alike. Some are simple monochrome dot-matrix printers, while others are full-color inkjet or laser printers capable of printing business cards, flyers, and digitized photographs with the utmost in clarity and resolution.

CD-ROM drives are becoming increasingly popular for storing databases, clip art, and programs too massive to fit comfortably on multiple high-density floppy disks. Even better, multimedia programs are appearing every day. These let people explore the sights and sounds of foreign countries, diagnose and treat common medical emergencies, and browse through entire collections of encyclopedias, classic novels, and reference dictionaries.

Because many of these CD-ROM programs include both video and sound, special sound cards and speakers will let you hear the full audio spectrum of classical music scores, wild animal cries, or even your own recorded voice.

For storing pictures and text, hand-held and flatbed scanners are becoming increasingly popular. With the right software, you can retouch digitized photographs or scan in pages of text to avoid typing it in yourself.

Of course, with such a variety of important and diverse data in your computer, it's crucial to have backup copies in case your computer should fail for any reason. To make backups easy, convenient, and automatic, many people install tape backup systems.

Necessary tools and equipment

To build your own computer, you'll need a flathead screwdriver and a Phillips head screwdriver along with a flat, clean surface on which to put everything. In addition, you may want several cups, bowls, or plastic bags to keep loose screws and small parts from rolling away.

Your work area should be clean and well-lit. Since you'll be plugging electronic equipment together, you may want an anti-static wristband to discharge any static electricity your body may build up. If you touch an electronic part and "shock" it with static electricity, the part could be ruined and you might have to throw it away.

Finally, your work area should include several electric outlets so you can plug everything in. Once you have prepared your work area, you're ready to get started.

Judging "green" products

When judging "green" computer products, it's important to use objective criteria for evaluating different parts. Throughout this book, you'll find products rated from one to four stars.

A four-star product meets the maximum level of computing "greenness." A one-star product meets the minimum level. Products can get a star if they meet the following:

- One star if it consumes less energy than ordinary parts and equipment.
- One star if it reduces or eliminates health hazards such as electromagnetic radiation or repetitive motion injuries.

- One star if it is built or packaged using recycled plastics, soy inks, unbleached paper, and other environment-saving materials.
- One star if the manufacturer is actively involved in large-scale recycling or donating to environmental causes.

Such a rating system helps you identify those truly "green" products and those products just jumping on the "green" bandwagon in hopes for a quick sale with "ecologically correct" advertising and marketing campaigns.

For example, a two-star monitor might meet the EPA Energy Star guidelines and reduce electromagnetic radiation, but the manufacturer doesn't use recycled materials or packaging and doesn't support any environmental causes.

Or a one-star computer might just meet the EPA Energy Star guidelines for reduced energy consumption, but ignore all the other criteria. While meeting EPA Energy Star guidelines is certainly a step in the right direction, it's a tiny step if other, "greener" options are available that offer similar prices and performance.

Throughout this book, products have been rated from one to four stars using these criteria. Just because a product only gets one or two stars doesn't necessarily mean that they don't use recycled materials or that they don't support environmental programs; it just means that the company doesn't actively advertise that fact. Green ratings in this book are basically conservative. The more stars a product receives, the more active that company has been in promoting their involvement with the environment.

If in doubt, contact a company directly and ask about their ecological policies. They may change between the time of this writing and the time you read this book.

How much will a "green" PC cost (or save)?

No matter how environmentally friendly a "green" computer may be, the ultimate question boils down to whether a green PC will save you the green that really counts: your money.

At the simplest level a green PC will cut your electricity bill. How much it does so depends on how often you use your computer. Heavy computer users might see savings anywhere from $150 to $200 a year, while infrequent computer users may see savings of $20 to $50 a year. Cutting your electricity bill may save you money in the future, but what about now?

Although prices fluctuate wildly and will likely be less by the time you read this, here are the specifications and the final cost for the green PC that I built for this book:

The green PC
- Desktop case (made from recycled plastics)
- 80486DX, 33 MHz
- "Green" motherboard with two VESA slots and six ISA slots
- 8MB RAM
- 128K built-in cache
- 340MB hard drive

- Combination 5.25- and 3.5-inch floppy drive
- VESA floppy/hard drive controller card
- Internal double-speed CD-ROM drive
- Labtec speakers and Spectrum 16-bit sound card
- 14-inch Energy Star monitor with 1024×768 resolution
- VESA graphics accelerator card with 1MB RAM
- Northgate OmniKey keyboard
- Generic ergonomic serial mouse
- Total Cost: $2,283.79 (December 1993)

If you had bought a complete computer through mail-order at this time, this is what you would have paid for a comparable system, according to the magazine advertisements in the December 21, 1993 edition of PC Magazine:

Gateway's mail-order PC
- Desktop case
- 80486DX2, 50 MHz
- Motherboard with two VESA slots and five ISA slots
- 8MB RAM
- 128K built-in cache
- 424MB hard drive
- One 3.5-inch floppy drive
- VESA floppy/hard drive controller card
- Internal double-speed CD-ROM drive
- 15-inch monitor
- VESA graphics accelerator card with 2Mb RAM
- Keyboard
- Microsoft mouse
- Choice of application software
- Total Cost: $2,295 (December 1993)

The Gateway computer offers a bigger hard disk, faster processor, and slightly larger monitor, while lacking speakers and a sound card.

Zeos International PC
- 80486DX2, 50 MHz
- 8MB RAM
- 128K built-in cache
- 426MB hard drive
- One 3.5-inch and one 5.25-inch floppy drive
- VESA floppy/hard drive controller card
- 14-inch monitor
- VESA graphics accelerator card with 1Mb RAM
- Keyboard
- Microsoft mouse
- Choice of application software from Lotus
- Total Cost: $2,295 (December 1993)

The Zeos computer offers a bigger hard disk and a faster processor, but lacks a sound card, speakers, and an internal CD-ROM disk drive. In addition, the Zeos computer ad (as advertised at the time) did not mention any compliance with the Energy Star criteria, nor does its monitor mention any MPR II low-emission compliance.

Austin Computers PC
- 80486DX2, 66 MHz
- 4MB RAM
- 340MB hard drive
- One 3.5-inch floppy drive
- VESA floppy/hard drive controller card
- Internal CD-ROM disk drive
- 14-inch monitor
- VESA graphics accelerator card with 512K RAM
- Speakers and MediaMagic 16-bit sound card
- Keyboard
- Microsoft mouse
- Energy Star compliant
- Total Cost: $2,349 (December 1993)

The Austin multimedia computer includes a CD-ROM drive, speakers, and a 16-bit sound card, but includes less memory on both the motherboard and the graphics card at a slightly higher price.

Gateway, Zeos, and Austin offer the lowest prices among the mail-order dealers, so you can see that building your own green PC meets or beats the prices from these cost-savings leaders. Local dealers will likely sell similar computers for slightly more. To compare the green PC to higher-priced mail-order dealers, look at the prices advertised by NCR and Dell Computers in the January 11, 1994 edition of PC Magazine.

NCR PC
- Desktop case
- 80486DX2, 50 MHz
- Motherboard with two VESA slots and four ISA slots
- 8MB RAM
- 240MB hard drive
- One 3.5-inch floppy drive
- VESA floppy/hard drive controller card
- 14-inch monitor
- VESA graphics accelerator card with 1Mb RAM
- Keyboard
- Microsoft mouse
- Total Cost: $2,320 (January 1994)

The NCR computer has a faster processor but fewer ISA slots, a smaller hard drive, and a higher price while lacking speakers, a sound card, an internal CD-ROM, and any mention of Energy Star compliance.

Dell Computers PC
- Desktop case
- 80486DX2, 50 MHz
- Motherboard with one VESA slots and five ISA slots
- 8MB RAM
- 128K built-in cache
- 320MB hard drive
- One 3.5-inch floppy drive
- VESA floppy/hard drive controller card
- Internal double-speed CD-ROM drive
- 15-inch Energy Star monitor with 1024 × 768 resolution
- VESA graphics accelerator card with 1Mb RAM
- Keyboard
- Microsoft mouse
- Total Cost: $2,499 (January 1994)

The Dell computer has a faster processor and a slightly larger monitor, but fewer expansion slots and a slightly smaller hard disk while lacking a 5.25-inch disk drive, speakers, and a sound card. The Dell computer also lacks any mention of Energy Star compliance.

By comparing the cost of building the green PC to different mail-order dealers, you can see that building your own green PC can save you as much money as buying from the least expensive mail-order dealer. Compared to a higher-priced mail-order dealer or local dealer, you might even save hundreds of dollars building your own computer.

Best of all, building your own computer teaches you how your computer works, lets you customize it exactly the way you want it for maximum "greenness," and gives you a sense of accomplishment when you put together something all by yourself. And that sense of "I did it myself" is something you can never get from buying a computer from somebody else.

Ten principles of "green" computing

When shopping for a "green" computer, here are some principles to keep in mind:
1. Save your money. Never pay more for a "green" computer part than for a non-green computer part. There's no sense going broke buying environmentally friendly equipment if there's something cheaper you could use instead. Unless you're more concerned with the environment than your pocketbook, make sure the first "green" you save is your own money.
2. Save electricity. Make sure your "green" computer parts save electricity. After the initial cost of the computer, your computer will continue costing you money in electrical bills. The more power-saving features your computer has (computer, monitor, printer, etc.) the less expensive it will be for you to use in the long run. This type of "green" savings won't always be obvious.
3. Protect your health. Part of green computing means having a computer that won't kill you through electromagnetic emissions or poorly designed keyboards. Pay a little bit more for comfort, even if it costs more than

similar equipment. (This contradicts principle #1. How you resolve the conflict is up to you.) In the long run, saving a few dollars now won't be worth the pain and agony you might experience later by using a poorly designed keyboard or mouse.

4. Support environmentally conscious companies. Buy from a company that uses recycled packaging or plastics in their equipment. Given the choice between a case made from virgin plastic or one made from recycled plastics, choose the recycled one as long as the price is similar. This type of shopping rewards those companies willing to make a commitment to saving the environment.

5. Support environmentally conscious dealers. Buy from a dealer (not from the manufacturer) whenever possible. Oddly enough, many manufacturers will charge full price for their equipment to avoid conflicting with their dealers. As a result, it's often cheaper to buy equipment through a dealer than go direct to the manufacturer. Again, buy from dealers that use recycled packaging over ones that don't.

6. Buy recycled products. Buy recycled or remanufactured paper, ribbons, or toner cartridges for your computer. There's no sense building a green computer if you wind up using virgin paper to print.

7. Recycle whenever possible. Don't throw away your old computer, floppy disks, manuals, or computer paper. Find a way to recycle it. Recycling doesn't mean driving ten miles out of your way to find a recycling center. Recycling can be as simple as giving your church or best friend your old computer or software, or it can be as sophisticated as finding a charitable organization that can use your computer.

8. Spread the word. Besides making your computer as green as possible, show others how they can save money by following green principles. Even people who couldn't care less about the environment will start caring if they can see how it can save them money.

9. Start today. You don't have to wait until you buy a brand new computer to start saving money and the environment. You can get started by just buying recycled paper, special energy-saving power strips that will reduce your computer's electricity consumption, or even just making a conscious effort to turn off your computer whenever you're not using it. Every little bit helps.

10. Think green. Once you've made your computer as green as possible, don't stop there. Think on ways to make your house, your transportation, your food, and everything else in your life more environmentally conscious. Not only will you be saving money, but you'll be helping protect the environment from needless destruction in all aspects of your life.

The current "green" standard

Perhaps the most environmentally friendly computer at the time of this writing is IBM's PS/2E computer. Here are some of its most prominent features, which you may want to duplicate or exceed when building your own green PC:

- Low-voltage (3.3 volts) IBM 80486SLC processor.
- Uses an external power supply (similar to those found in laptops), which eliminates the need for a cooling fan.
- Computer case made from recycled plastics that snaps apart for easy disassembly.
- Small size, allowing it to take up less desk space than ordinary computer cases.
- Hard/floppy drive controller built-in on the motherboard.
- Liquid crystal color display that's completely emission-free.
- Uses PCMCIA cards instead of ordinary expansion cards to save space. In addition, PCMCIA cards require less material to make than ordinary expansion cards.
- Includes the TrackPoint II pointing device built-in to the keyboard, eliminating the need for a separate mouse or trackball.
- A detachable numeric keypad lets users adjust its position for maximum comfort, whether you're a right- or left-handed user.

IBM's PS/2E represents the latest technology for creating a green PC. By keeping the features of the PS/2E in mind, you can see how the green PC that you plan to build compares. If you're interested in saving money and building a green PC, your green PC will likely fall short of the IBM PS/2E. However, if money is no object, your green PC could possible equal or surpass the IBM PS/2E in environmental friendliness. What your green PC turns out to be depends entirely on what's important to you.

Deciding what you need

What do you need in a computer? Speed? Storage? Cost? Size? Future expandability? Do you plan to use your computer for desktop publishing or database management? Spreadsheet analysis or just playing games?

Whatever your needs might be, they'll affect the type of equipment you need to consider. Someone interested in desktop publishing needs a more expensive monitor and video card than someone interested in word processing or database management.

Throughout this book, you'll find checklists to identify what types of parts are best for you. No two people use a computer exactly the same way. By identifying those areas most important to you and those you couldn't care less about, you'll truly have a machine that you can call a personal computer.

How this book is organized

The first half of this book describes each part of the computer in more detail, explaining the different options available, what features to look for, and which brand names provide the most "green" capabilities. In addition, this part of the book also includes several checklists to help you decide which type of equipment is best for your needs.

For example, if you want to build the fastest computer possible, you'll need to look for certain features in motherboards, hard disks, and even monitors. If speed is less important than cost, then you can safely ignore or overlook many options that you will never use.

The second half of this book gives step-by-step explanations for putting your computer together. This part also contains troubleshooting procedures for testing your computer, along with a list of common problems that can go wrong with each piece of equipment. This part also contains tips for creating and modifying your AU-TOEXEC.BAT and CONFIG.SYS files, enhancing your computer's performance with utility programs, and protecting your hard disk from virus attacks.

If you want to convert an existing computer into a "green" PC, Appendix A lists several products you can buy to reduce your computer's energy requirements. While such a converted "green" PC won't be as efficient as a "green" PC built entirely out of "green" parts, it can be a quick and inexpensive solution to preserve your current computer equipment.

No matter how much you may love your current computer, eventually there'll come a time when it will be less expensive to buy a brand new computer and put the old one aside. Rather than throw the old computer away, Appendix B lists various computer recycling organizations that take old equipment and distribute it to charities around the world. Even if your old computer isn't "green," you can still reduce its impact on the environment by letting others continue to use it rather than throwing it away and contributing to a landfill.

Appendix C lists resources for learning more about "green" computing and environmental issues in general. Such resources are magazines, books, on-line services, and groups actively involved in protecting our natural resources.

Throughout this book you'll find plenty of product names, addresses, and phone numbers of "green" computer products. Just keep in mind that a listing in this book is not an endorsement or recommendation of any kind. Certain companies are listed here because they're part of the "green" PC movement, and it's highly possible that other companies should be listed but are not.

If you know of a company or product that deserves mention in this book, feel free to contact me at CompuServe 70334,3672. I'll make sure that all relevant companies and products get listed in future editions.

Whether you plan to build your own computer, upgrade your current one, or just learn more about "green" computing, the information and product listings I've provided should get you started in the right direction. Whatever your current knowledge and computer skills may be, you'll find something in this book for everyone.

2
Motherboards

The motherboard is the main circuit board that the other parts of the computer attach or plug into. Motherboards contain four crucial items that determine the capability of your entire computer:
- The central processing unit (CPU)
- The expansion bus
- The basic input/output system (BIOS)
- The maximum amount of random access memory (RAM)

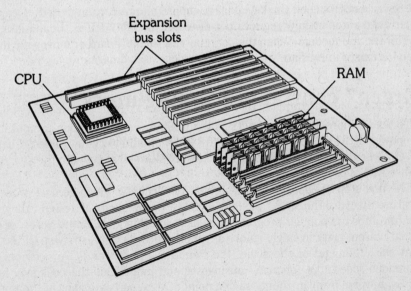

2-1 A typical motherboard.

What to look for in a "green" motherboard

There are two types of "green" motherboards available: "light green" and "dark green." A "light green" motherboard consists of standard parts, with the addition of a keyboard controller that automatically reduces power when no one touches the keyboard or mouse. The most popular "green" keyboard controller is the American Megatrends International (AMI) MegaKey. Many motherboard manufacturers use the MegaKey as a quick way to convert existing motherboards into "green" PCs.

MegaKey enhanced motherboards meet the bare minimum power requirements of the Energy Star program. However, a better choice are "dark green" motherboards, which are designed using low-voltage microprocessors, special Basic Input/Output System (BIOS) chips to control power use, "green" chipsets, and motherboards manufactured without using toxic chemicals such as lead-oxide or chlorofluorocarbons (CFCs). "Dark green" motherboards follow Intel's System Management Mode (SMM) specifications for power conservation.

Given the choice between similarly priced "light green" and "dark green" motherboards, it's easy to see that "dark green" motherboards are more energy efficient and environmentally friendly. To identify the difference between "light green" and "dark green" motherboards, find out how the motherboard meets the Energy Star requirements. If it uses the MegaKey chip, then it's a "light green" motherboard. If it uses SMM, it may still be a "light green" motherboard (still made with toxic chemicals) or it might be a "dark green" motherboard (made without toxic chemicals). To determine if a motherboard is made using toxic chemicals, you'll have to contact the motherboard manufacturer.

Both the MegaKey and SMM methods of power conservation work the same way. If the user hasn't touched the keyboard or mouse after a certain period of time, the motherboard automatically reduces power to peripherals such as the monitor, hard disk, printer, and modem. When the user touches the keyboard or moves the mouse, the motherboard immediately turns these devices back on again.

"Green" central processing units

The central processing unit acts as the brain or engine of your computer. The more powerful the CPU, the more powerful your computer will be. Table 2-1 lists the different types of CPUs available, from fastest to slowest, along with the advantages and disadvantages of each.

The first step in choosing a motherboard is deciding which central processing unit to use. Because the 80286 and 8086/8088 CPUs are such old designs, they won't run most of today's popular programs like Microsoft Windows, Lotus Notes, or OS/2. For that reason, you can safely ignore any motherboards that use these CPUs.

At the other end of the scale, the Pentium and Power PC processors offer tremendous speed, but for many businesses and individuals the cost may be too high. Even worse from an energy-saving point of view, early versions of the Pentium operate at 5 volts, instead of the power-saving standard of 3.3 volts that consumes up to 60% less electricity. So if you decide to choose a Pentium motherboard, wait until Intel releases a 3.3 low-voltage version.

Table 2-1. Comparison of different central processing units

CPU name	Advantages	Disadvantages
PowerPC	Faster than Intel's Pentium processor at roughly half the price.	Not likely to be available until late 1994. Compatibility with existing IBM software is questionable.
Pentium	Latest "standard" for IBM compatibility. More than twice as fast than the 80486 processor. Uses System Management Mode (SMM) to meet the Energy Star guidelines for power use.	Expensive and in short supply. Early versions only operate at 5 volts, instead of 3.3 volts.
80486	Current "standard" for IBM compatibility. Special versions use System Management Mode (SMM) to meet the Energy Star guidelines for power use.	May be too expensive for personal use. Not all versions of this processor take advantage of SMM to reduce power consumption.
80386	Previous "standard" for IBM compatibility. Inexpensive and plentiful.	May be too slow for running certain types of programs. Fast becoming obsolete. Not all versions of this processor take advantage of SMM to reduce power consumption.
80286	Inexpensive and plentiful.	Won't run most of the newer programs. Obsolete for most business use.
8086/8088	Inexpensive but scarce.	Won't run most of the newer programs. Obsolete for most business and personal use.

When considering 80386 and 80486 processors, look for the special 3.3 low-voltage versions that have the designations 80486DLC, 80486SLC, 80486SL, 80386DLC, 80386SLC, and 80386SL. The "L" designation in the name means that it's a "low power" processor. The "C" designation in the name means that it comes with a built-in cache for faster processing. A cache can make a processor run faster by temporarily storing information from memory. The larger the cache size, the faster the processor can run. Typical sizes for internal caches are 1K, 2K, 8K, and 16K.

The "D" and "S" designation refers to the two different versions of the same processor. For example, an 80486DX processor includes a built-in math coprocessor, but an 80486SX processor does not. If speedy numerical calculations are important, then look for processors with the "D" designation.

Table 2-2 shows the equivalent processors to these DLC, DL, SLC and SL processors with the fastest processor at the top of the list and the slowest one at the bottom.

The 80486DLC processor is the fastest, but also the most expensive. The 80386SL processor may be the slowest, but it's the least expensive. To make matters even more confusing, even identical processors may run at different speeds; chip speed is measured in megahertz (MHz). For example, some 80386SLC processors run at 20 MHz while others run at 25 MHz. Common processor speeds include 16 MHz, 20 MHz, 25 MHz, 33 MHz, 40 MHz, 50 MHz, and 66 MHz.

Table 2-2. Comparison of DLC and SLC processors

CPU name	Equivalent to	Comments
80486DLC	80486DX	
80486SLC	80486SX	Lacks a math co-processor
8046SL	80486SX	Lacks a built-in cache
80386DLC	80386DX	
80386SLC	80386SX	Lacks a math co-processor
80386SL	80386SX	Lacks a built-in cache

You can buy a motherboard and CPU separately, but most motherboards come with CPUs already installed. When buying a motherboard, check to see which company makes the processor. The most popular processors are made by Intel, IBM, Cyrix, and American Micro Devices (AMD). Table 2-3 lists the processors these companies make along their "green" rating.

Table 2-3. Green ratings of different CPU manufacturers

Company	Processor	"Green" rating	
Motorola	PowerPC	*	(One star for energy conserving features)
Intel	Pentium (3.3-volt version)	*	(One star for energy conserving features)
	80486DLC	*	
	80486DL	*	
	80386SLC	*	
	80386SL	*	
IBM	80486SLC	***	(One star for energy conserving features)
	80386SLC		(One star for in-house recycling)
			(One star for supporting environmental research)
Cyrix	80486DLC	**	(One star for energy conserving features)
	80486SLC	**	
	80386DLC	**	(One star for in-house recycling)
	80386SLC	**	
AMD	Am80486DXLV	**	(One star for energy conserving features)
	Am80486SXLV	**	
	Am80386 DXLV	**	(One star for in-house recycling)
	Am80386SXLV	**	

The use of a low-voltage microprocessor alone is no guarantee that the motherboard meets the Energy Star requirements. To work properly, a motherboard must include a "green" BIOS chip and a" green" chipset. The BIOS chip contains instructions that mimic the original IBM BIOS chip, ensuring compatibility with software and hardware designed for IBM computers. The chipset coordinates the activities of all the computer parts, ensuring that they work correctly.

The three most popular "green" BIOS chips are the Award 4.5 Elite Series BIOS, Phoenix BIOS 4.0, and AMI Green BIOS. These BIOS chips work with many of the "green" chipsets available. The combination of a "green" BIOS chip, "green" chipsets, and low-voltage processors creates the "greenest" motherboard possible.

Since motherboards are usually sold with the microprocessor, BIOS chip, and chipset already installed, it's easier to look for those motherboards already designated as "green" motherboards rather than trying to identify individual "green" parts. Just make sure any" green" motherboard you get contains these three elements:

- A low-voltage microprocessor (3.3-volt)
- A "green" BIOS chip
- A "green" chipset

Zero insertion force (ZIF) sockets

Once you buy most motherboards, you're usually stuck with the processor that came with it. If you want to upgrade your computer, you can only plug in a faster version of the same processor. For example, a motherboard designed for an 80486DX processor can only use another 80486DX processor. Because the number of pins used by the 80486DX and the Pentium processor differs, you can never plug a Pentium into a motherboard that uses an 80486DX processor (or an 80486DX processor into an 80386DX motherboard).

An exception to this is the Cx486DRx2 processor, which is a specially designed 80486 processor that's designed to fit into an ordinary 80386 processor socket. However, the cost of buying a new 80386 motherboard and using a Cx486DRx2 processor may be almost equal to the cost of buying a new 80486 motherboard.

However, certain 80486DX motherboards offer a special socket called a zero insertion force (ZIF) socket. These sockets come with extra pin holes, letting you plug in a more advanced processor at a future date.

To remove your old 80486DX processor, you just pull a lever at the side of the socket, pull out the processor, drop a new Pentium processor in the socket, and push the lever back down to hold the new processor in place. The entire procedure takes less than five minutes.

Of course, not all motherboards offer this feature. If you hope to upgrade your 80486 processor to a Pentium processor some time in the future, make sure your motherboard includes a zero insertion force socket.

Should you buy a math coprocessor?

Generally, the answer is no. If you plan to use a computer for computer-aided design or intense scientific, engineering, or financial calculations, then speed will be a top priority, and you should choose a Pentium or 80486DX. Both come with a math coprocessor built-in.

If numerical calculations aren't that important to you, then the cost of a math coprocessor will be hard to justify. For word processing or database management, a math coprocessor will be next to worthless. For spreadsheet analysis or other types of graphics, a math coprocessor may make your computer run faster, but not always noticeably so.

A math coprocessor even destroys the one advantage of the 80486SX processor, which is its lower cost. If you buy an 80486SX and a 80487SX math coprocessor, you essentially have the same capabilities of an 80486DX processor, but at a higher cost and a slower operating speed.

If you decide to buy an 80386DX or 80386SX processor, adding a math co-processor can be almost as expensive as buying an 80486DX right from the start. But if you're buying or building a new computer and you don't need the capabilities of a Pentium or 80486DX, then you probably don't need a math coprocessor either.

The expansion bus

After the CPU, the second most important feature of a motherboard is the type of expansion bus it uses. An expansion bus lets you add new features to your computer by plugging in new expansion cards. The more expansion slots a motherboard offers, the more expansion cards you can plug in. Unfortunately, the capabilities of expansion buses vary, and not all expansion cards plug into all types of expansion buses.

The most common expansion bus is ISA, which stands for Industry Standard Architecture. The ISA expansion buses are the slowest, but since this standard has been around since 1981, you can find plenty of expansion cards to choose from at extremely low prices.

The next type of expansion bus is called EISA, which stands for Extended Industry Standard Architecture. An EISA bus lets you plug in expansion cards designed for the ISA bus as well as expansion cards designed for the EISA bus. (Note: You cannot plug EISA expansion cards into an ISA bus.)

The EISA standard appeared in 1987 when IBM developed a new bus design called the Micro Channel Architecture (MCA). Although the MCA bus offered better performance than the old ISA bus, the MCA bus required different types of expansion cards. Even worse, IBM required other manufacturers to pay them royalties for any MCA buses they developed in clone computers, or any MCA-compatible expansion cards.

Not surprisingly, few companies were willing to follow this new standard, and several major computer manufacturers, including AST Research, Compaq, Epson, Hewlett-Packard, and Zenith, banded together and developed the EISA standard. Although the EISA expansion bus runs faster than the ISA expansion bus, not many companies make EISA expansion cards. As a result, the EISA expansion bus standard hasn't been as widely adopted as was originally hoped. Given the higher cost of an EISA motherboard, more people are buying ISA motherboards that use a local bus instead.

Local buses

The latest motherboards now include something called a local bus. In the early days, both the ISA and EISA buses worked fine. But as color graphic standards improved, networks appeared, and faster hard disks were introduced, both the ISA and

EISA buses were simply too slow to keep up with faster data transfer. To fix this problem, manufacturers developed local buses.

A local bus works with an ISA or EISA bus and takes care of data transfer between the CPU and any peripherals, like hard disks, networks, and monitors. The two most common local bus designs are the VESA local bus (sometimes abbreviated as VESA bus or VL-bus) and the PCI local bus.

The VESA (Video Electronics Standards Association) local bus was developed primarily to handle faster and more complex graphic images. Since this standard has been around since 1992, you can find plenty of video cards and other types of expansion cards that plug into a VESA local bus. The main drawback of a VESA local bus is that it only offers a maximum of three expansion slots: one for a video card, one for a hard drive/floppy drive controller card, and one for a network adapter card.

The PCI (Peripheral Component Interconnect) local bus was developed by Intel as a local bus designed to handle more than just graphics. A PCI local bus can transfer data much faster than a VESA local bus, but because the PCI standard is so new, there are few PCI expansion cards that work with it. As a result, motherboards offering the PCI local bus will be more expensive than motherboards offering the VESA local bus.

If you're trying to minimize costs, a VESA local bus motherboard will be less expensive. Best of all, VESA local bus expansion cards are plentiful and inexpensive as well. But for long-term compatibility, consider the PCI local bus. Even Apple Computers plans to adapt the PCI local bus for their new breed of Macintosh computers. In the future, PCI local bus expansion cards will become as plentiful and inexpensive as VESA local bus expansion cards.

Bus configurations

When shopping for motherboards, look to see which types of buses the motherboard offers and how many expansion slots are available on each bus. To offer as much compatibility as possible, many motherboards offer a combination of two different buses, an ISA or EISA bus and a VESA or PCI local bus. Table 2-4 lists the different types of expansion buses available from fastest (top) to slowest (bottom).

Table 2-4. Typical motherboard bus configurations

Motherboard bus configurations	Comments
PCI EISA	Can use PCI, EISA, and ISA expansion cards.
VESA EISA	Can use VESA, EISA, and ISA expansion cards
VESA ISA	Can use VESA and ISA expansion cards
EISA	Can use EISA or ISA expansion cards
ISA	Can only use ISA expansion cards

Random access memory (RAM)

As a general rule, the more memory a computer has, the faster it will run. Depending on the type of programs you plan to use, you may need anywhere from 4MB up to 16MB or beyond. Microsoft Windows requires at least 2MB to run although 4MB is recommended and 8MB is the norm. OS/2 requires at least 4MB to run although 8MB or more is common. In any case, the more RAM, the more programs your computer can use.

Unfortunately, all motherboards have a maximum limit on the amount of RAM you can plug directly into the motherboard. This maximum RAM limit can be 16MB, 32MB, 64MB, or 128MB. If you need to add more memory than your motherboard can handle, you'll have to buy an expensive memory expansion card.

Although two motherboards may provide the same amount of memory, they may use one of two types of memory chips called Single In-Line Memory Modules (SIMMs) or Single In-Line Pin Packages (SIPPs). Of the two, SIMMs are becoming more popular and commonplace. Both SIMMs and SIPPs are memory chips grouped together for convenience and come in sizes ranging from 1MB to 4MB. Basically, the only difference between the two is the way they plug into the motherboard. Neither type of memory chip is interchangeable with the other, so if your motherboard uses SIMMs, you can't plug in SIPPs and vice versa.

Memory chips (SIMMs and SIPPs) are also rated according to speed, measured in nanoseconds (ns). Most memory chips run at 70 ns, although 60 ns, 50 ns, and 40 ns speeds are common (and more expensive). Although you can use memory chips that run at slower speeds, your computer will be forced to run slower as well.

Cache

Some motherboards come with a built-in cache, which is a special group of memory chips whose sole function in life is to make your computer faster. (Note that this motherboard cache is separate from any cache your CPU might have built-in.) Accessing data from a floppy or hard disk all the time slows down your computer. A cache simply grabs data off the floppy or hard disk while the computer is doing something else, and then quickly hands this data to the processor when it needs it. By accessing the cache instead of the floppy or hard disk, the computer can run faster.

Typical cache sizes are 64K, 128K, and 256K. The larger the cache, the more data it can hold and the faster your computer will run. If speed isn't that important, get a motherboard with no cache or a 64K cache. If speed is important, then get a 128K or 256K cache.

Note that some motherboards may have a 128K or 256K cache, but only have 64K of memory plugged into it. If you want to expand your cache size, you just have to add more memory chips.

Extra items included on the motherboard

All other factors being equal, the "greenest" motherboard is one that uses the fewest materials. Some of the latest motherboards now offer a built-in IDE controller, mouse port, and serial/parallel ports.

With most motherboards, an IDE controller and serial/parallel ports require a separate expansion card, using up an expansion slot, costing you extra money, and using additional materials to make. Although motherboards with built-in features are slightly more expensive than "bare-bones" motherboards without any built-in features, compare costs carefully.

By the time you buy a "bare-bones" motherboard and add in the cost for a separate IDE controller card and serial/parallel port card, the total cost could be equal or greater than a motherboard with these features already built-in.

Deciphering motherboard advertisements

With all of this information about BIOS, RAM, SIMMs, CPUs, and nanoseconds spinning through your head, how can you compare what you want to what you can buy? Here are some sample ads from a typical computer magazine, along with their English translations.

"486DLC 3-VESA 256K P24T socket"

- An 80486DLC processor
- A VESA local bus with three VESA bus expansion slots
- A 256K cache
- A ZIF socket for upgrading your processor to a more advanced processor at a future date

"486DLC-33 Cyrix 256K 3-EISA 2-VESA LB"

- An 80486DLC processor made by Cyrix, that runs at a maximum speed of 33 MHz
- A 256K cache
- An EISA bus with three expansion slots
- A VESA local bus with two expansion slots

"486/50, AMI, PCI Local Bus, 128K cache w/o CPU"

- A socket for an 80486 processor, running at 50 MHz
- An AMI BIOS chip
- A PCI local bus
- A 128K cache

"386SL, ISA, 256K cache, AMI BIOS, MAX 128MB"

- An 80386SL processor
- An ISA expansion bus

- A 256K cache
- An AMI BIOS chip
- A maximum of 128Mb RAM that you can plug directly into the motherboard

"486DLC 5-ISA, 3-EISA, 2-VESA 256K, P-24T Ready"

- An 80486DLC processor
- An expansion bus with 3 EISA expansion slots, 5 ISA expansion slots, and 2 VESA Local bus expansion slots
- A 256K cache
- A ZIF socket for upgrading your processor to a more advanced processor at a future date

Unfortunately, motherboard advertisements are neither standard nor complete. One ad might advertise "ZIF socket" while another might just say "P24T Ready." In both cases, this means that the motherboard has a ZIF socket for upgrading to a more advanced processor, like the Pentium, at a later date.

Even worse, ads by themselves can be deceptive. When an ad says that a motherboard has a "2 VESA," you know that this means the motherboard has a VESA local bus with 2 expansion slots, but you have no idea of knowing whether the accompanying expansion bus is an ISA or EISA type.

When shopping for a motherboard, make sure that you know exactly what features you're buying. Not all motherboard advertisements will mention any "green" capabilities, so ask your dealer to answer any questions the ads might not tell you. To help you shop for a motherboard, use the following checklist as a guideline.

Motherboard shopping checklist

Power management system used:
- ❏ MegaKeySystem
- ❏ Management Mode (SMM)

Processor type:
- ❏ PowerPC
- ❏ 80486DLC
- ❏ 80486SL
- ❏ 80386DL
- ❏ Pentium
- ❏ 80486SLC
- ❏ 80386DLC
- ❏ 80386SLC

Processor manufacturer:
- ❏ Intel
- ❏ IBM
- ❏ Motorola
- ❏ Cyrix
- ❏ American Micro Devices (AMD)

Processor speed:
- ❏ 66 MHz
- ❏ 33 MHz
- ❏ 20 MHz
- ❏ 50 MHz
- ❏ 25 MHz
- ❏ 16 MHz

Zero insertion force socket: ❏ Yes   ❏ No

Expansion bus: ❏ EISA   Number of EISA expansion slots: _____
                     ❏ ISA   Number of ISA expansion slots: _____

Local bus: ❏ PCI   Number of PCI expansion slots: _____
                 ❏ VESA Number of VESA expansion slots: _____
                 ❏ None

**Maximum
RAM available:**
                 ❏ 128MB   ❏ 64MB
                 ❏ 32MB   ❏ 16MB

**RAM included
on motherboard:**
                 ❏ 128MB   ❏ 64MB
                 ❏ 32MB   ❏ 16MB
                 ❏ 8MB   ❏ 4MB
                 ❏ 2MB   ❏ 1MB

Cache size: ❏ 256 K   ❏ 128 K
                  ❏ 64K   ❏ None

BIOS Chip manufacturer: ❏ AMI   ❏ Phoenix
                              ❏ Award   ❏ Other _____

Warranty: ❏ 3 Year   ❏ 2 Year
                ❏ 1 Year   ❏ 30 Days

Dealer:

_____

Price:

_____

    The following lists various "green" motherboard and BIOS chip manufacturers. Although some of these manufacturers won't sell parts directly to individuals, they can refer you to other manufacturers who use their parts, as well as to any local or mail-order distributors who sell "green" motherboards.

"Green" BIOS chip manufacturers

AMI Green BIOS
MegaKey Keyboard Controller
American Megatrends International
6145-F Northbelt Parkway
Nocross, GA 30071
Tel: (404) 263-8181
Fax: (404) 263-9381

Award 4.5 Elite Series BIOS
Award Software International
777 E. Middlefield Road
Mountain View, CA 94043
Tel: (415) 968-0274
Fax: (415) 968-0274
BBS: (415) 968-0249

PhoenixBIOS 4.0
Phoenix Technologies
846 University Avenue
Norwood, MA 02062-3950
Tel: (617) 551-4000
Fax: (617) 551-3750

"Green" processor manufacturers

American Micro Devices, Inc. (AMD)
901 Thompson Place
P.O. Box 3453
Sunnyvale, CA 94088-3453
Tel: (408) 732-2400

Cyrix Corporation
2703 North Central Expressway
Richardson, TX 75080
Tel: (214) 994-8387
Fax: (214) 699-9857

IBM Microelectronics Division
Route 100
Somers, NY 10589
Tel: (800) IBM-0181

Intel Corporation
2200 Mission College Blvd.
Santa Clara, CA 95052-8119
Tel: (408) 765-8080
Fax: (503) 629-7580
BBS: (503) 645-6275

"Green" motherboard manufacturers

Cache Computers
46600 Landing Parkway
Fremont, CA 94538
Tel: (510) 226-9922
Fax: (510) 226-9911

Chicony America, Inc.
53 Parker
Irvine, CA 92718
Tel: (714) 380-0928
Fax: (714) 380-9204

Dataexpert Corporation
1156 Sonora Court
Sunnyvale, CA 94086
Tel: (408) 737-8880
Fax: (408) 737-8390

DD & TT Enterprise
5680 Rickenbacker Road
Bell, CA 90201
Tel: (213) 780-0099
Fax: (213) 780-0419

Destiny Computers
3480 Investment Boulevard
Hayward, CA 94545
Tel: (510) 783-2727
Fax: (510) 783-3003

DFI-USA
135 Main Avenue
Sacramento, CA 96838
Tel: (916) 568-1234
Fax: (916) 568-1233

Hokkins Systemation, Inc.
131 East Brokaw Road
San Jose, CA 95112
Tel: (408) 436-8303
Fax: (408) 436-3021

Leadertech Systems of Chicago, Inc.
2600 Greenleaf Avenue
Elk Grove Village, IL 60007
Tel: (708) 806-6262
Fax: (708) 806-6278

Meccer Corporation
29560 Union City Blvd.
Union City, CA 94587
Tel: (510) 475-5730
Fax: (510) 475-0982

Micronics Computers, Inc.
232 East Warren Avenue
Fremont, CA 94539
Tel: (510) 651-2300
Fax: (510) 651-5612

First International Computer
5020 Brandin Court
Fremont, CA 94538
Tel: (510) 683-9200
Fax: (510) 252-7777

MGV International, Inc.
451 Lanier Road
Madison, AL 35758
Tel: (205) 772-1100
Fax: (205) 772-1198

Praefa Technology, Inc.
148 S. 8th Avenue, Suite J
La Puente, CA 91746
Tel: (818) 336-8999
Fax: (818) 336-2999

Shuttle Computer International, Inc.
1161 Cadillac Court
Milpitas, CA 95035
Tel: (408) 945-1480
Fax: (408) 945-1481

Silicon Star International, Inc.
47889 Fremont Blvd.
Fremont, CA 94538
Tel: (510) 623-0500
Fax: (510) 623-1092

Summit Micro Design, Inc.
485 Macara Avenue, Suite 901
Sunnyvale, CA 94086
Tel: (408) 739-6348
Fax: (408) 739-4643

Sys Technology, Inc.
10655 Humbolt Street
Los Alamitos, CA 90720
Tel: (310) 493-6888
Fax: (310) 493-2816

TMC Research Corporation
631 S. Milpitas Blvd.
Milpitas, CA 95035
Tel: (408) 262-0888
Fax: (408) 262-1082

3
Floppy disk drives

Every computer needs at least one floppy disk drive, but what makes one floppy drive "greener" than another? When comparing floppy drives (like other types of computer parts) look at the amount of electricity they consume and the amount of material required to make them.

The latest floppy drives consume very little power, or combine a 5.25-inch and a 3.5-inch disk drive in one drive bay. For maximum "greenness," a floppy drive should connect to a hard/floppy controller built into your motherboard. Such a built-in controller eliminates the need for a separate controller card, thereby conserving material; although an even "greener" solution might be to eliminate the floppy disk drive altogether, don't do it.

For many people, the most convenient way to transfer files from one computer to another is through a floppy disk. When you buy a new program, it comes on several floppy disks so you can install it on your hard disk.

So no matter what you may read about the wonders of CD-ROM or the massive storage capacities of multi-gigabyte hard drives, you still need at least one floppy disk drive so you can share data with the rest of the world. The biggest problem lies in deciding which type of floppy disk drive to buy.

Types of floppy disks

Basically, floppy disks come in two sizes: 3.5 inch and 5.25 inch. Although more computers use 3.5-inch floppies because they're smaller and hold more data, the ancient 5.25-inch floppies are cheaper and more numerous because people have been using them since 1981.

Besides size, floppy disks are also available in different densities, which determine how much data they can hold. Table 3-1 shows the different types of floppy disks you can buy, along with the abbreviations used to identify them.

Table 3-1. Different types of floppy disks

Disk size	Disk type	Storage capacity
5.25-inch	Single-Sided/Double-Density (SS/DD)	180K
5.25-inch	Double-Sided/Double-Density (DS/DD)	360K
5.25-inch	High- or Quad-Density (HD)	1.2MB
3.5-inch	Double-Sided/Double-Density (DS/DD)	720K
3.5-inch	High- or Quad-Density (HD)	1.44MB
3.5-inch	Extended Density (ED)	2.88MB

The ancient 5.25-inch, single-sided/double-density floppy disks are completely obsolete, but some people may still have data stored on these types of disks. Likewise, the 5.25-inch and 3.5-inch, double-sided/double-density floppy disks are slowly being phased out, although many people still use them for making backup copies or archiving seldom-used files.

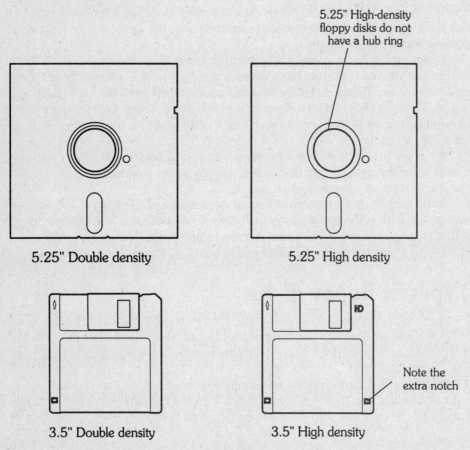

3-1 How to identify different types of floppy disks.

When you buy a program nowadays, it's likely to come on both 5.25-inch and 3.5-inch high-density floppy disks. Unfortunately, the 2.88MB floppy disk isn't very common and won't likely become popular for another year or two. As a result, few people can use 2.88MB floppy disks and almost no software publishers distribute programs on these types of disks.

Types of floppy disk drives

Because people still use so many floppy disk sizes and types, your computer should have two floppy drives for maximum compatibility:

- A 5.25-inch high-density (HD), 1.2MB drive
- A 3.5-inch high-density (HD), 1.44MB drive

A 5.25-inch high-density drive can use all types of 5.25-inch floppy disks, including the old single-sided/double-density types. A 3.5-inch high-density drive can use all types of 3.5-inch floppy disks except for the newest 2.88MB floppy disks. Table 3-2 lists the types of floppy disk drives available and the types of floppy disks they can use.

Table 3-2. Floppy disk drives

Floppy disk drive type	Floppy disks it can use
5.25-inch, 360K drive	180K (SS/DD)
	360K (DS/DD)
5.25-inch, 1.2MB drive	180K (SS/DD)
	360K (DS/DD)
	1.2MB (HD)
3.5-inch, 720K drive	720K (DS/DD)
3.5-inch, 1.44MB drive	720K (DS/DD)
	1.44MB (HD)
3.5-inch, 2.88MB drive	720K (DS/DD)
	1.44MB (HD)
	2.88MB (ED)

If space is tight, you could eliminate the 1.2MB floppy drive and just use a 1.44MB floppy drive instead. This might prove inconvenient at first, because you won't be able to share data stored on 5.25-inch floppy disks. But because most people are using the 3.5-inch floppy disks, this could cause less of a problem than you might think.

In case you want to save space, but still want to maintain compatibility with both floppy disk sizes, many companies make a combination 5.25-inch/3.5-inch floppy drive that fits in the same amount of space as one ordinary 1.2MB or 1.44MB floppy drive.

These dual floppy drive units cost slightly more than buying separate 1.2MB and 1.44MB floppy drives, but the savings in space may be worth it.

3-2 A combination 5.25-inch and 3.5-inch disk drive.

Floptical Disks

For users who store lots of data (such as graphics) on floppy disks, consider a 3.5-inch, 21MB floptical disk drive. These floptical disk drives can read and write to standard 3.5-inch 720K and 1.44MB floppy disks, as well as special 21MB floptical disks. Of course, these floptical disks cost about $10 to $15 apiece, and the floptical drives cost several hundred dollars.

Several companies make 21MB floptical disk drives, including Insite Peripherals, GrassRoots, and Iomega Corporation. Because few people have a floptical disk drive, the most common use for floptical disks is for backing up files or storing sensitive information on disks that you can pull out of the computer and lock up afterwards.

Floppy drive controller cards

Every floppy drive must have a floppy drive controller card. The floppy drive controller card tells the computer how to read and write data off the floppy drive. There are three options for buying a floppy drive controller card:

- Buy a dedicated floppy drive controller card.
- Buy a combination hard drive/floppy drive controller card.
- Buy a motherboard with a built-in floppy drive controller card.

A dedicated floppy drive controller card is generally wasteful because it takes up one expansion slot in your computer and only performs a single function. Because of this, dedicated floppy drive controller cards are rare.

More common are combination hard drive/floppy drive controller cards. This type of controller card typically can control two hard disks and four floppy drives. To further save space, some of these controller cards even include a serial or parallel port.

Even better than a combination hard drive/floppy drive controller card, some motherboards have a floppy drive controller built-in. With these types of motherboards, you can save the added expense of buying a separate controller card, plus keep an expansion slot open for future expansion cards.

Unfortunately, combination hard drive/floppy drive controller cards and controller cards built-in to motherboards usually work only with 360K, 1.2MB, 720K,

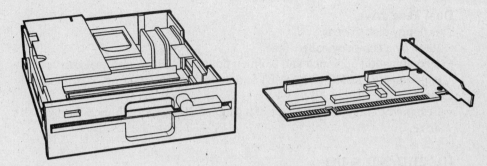

3-3 A typical floppy disk drive and controller card setup.

1.44MB, and 2.88MB floppy disk drives. If you want to use a 21MB floptical disk drive, you'll have to buy a dedicated floptical drive controller card.

Deciphering floppy disk and controller ads

Unlike motherboard advertisements, floppy disk drive advertisements are usually much simpler. The following lists typical advertisements along with their English translations:

Chinon 3.5" 1.44MB floppy drive
This floppy disk drive is:
- Made by a company called Chinon.
- Designed to use both 3.5-inch high-density (1.44MB) and double-density (720K) floppy disks.

1.2MB FD drive
This floppy disk drive is:
- Designed to use both 5.25-inch high-density (1.2MB) and double-density (360K) floppy disks.

Dual 1.2/1.44MB FD drive, Teac
This floppy disk drive is:
- Made by a company called Teac.
- A combination 5.25-inch and 3.5-inch floppy disk drive unit that can use high-density (1.2MB or 1.44MB) or double-density (360K or 720K) floppy disks.
- Designed to take up the space of a single 5.25-inch or 3.5-inch floppy disk drive.

Mitsumi 3.5" 2.88MB Ivory
This floppy disk drive is:
- Made by a company called Mitsumi.
- Designed to use 3.5-inch extended density (2.88MB), high-density (1.44MB), and double-density (720K) floppy disks.
- Ivory-colored.

Dual Teac drive

This floppy disk drive is:

- Made by a company called Teac.
- A combination 5.25-inch and 3.5-inch floppy disk drive unit that can use high-density (1.2MB or 1.44MB) or double-density (360K or 720K) floppy disks.
- Designed to take up the space of a single 5.25-inch or 3.5-inch floppy disk drive.

IDE 2HD/2FD & I/O

This controller card:

- Can control up to two IDE hard disks and two floppy disk drives.
- Has a serial and/or parallel port.

VESA IDE hard/floppy I/O card for 33/66 MHz

This controller card:

- Plus into a VESA local bus expansion slot.
- Can control an IDE hard disk and floppy disk drives.
- Has a serial and/or parallel port.
- Is designed to work with motherboards that run at 33 or 66 MHz.

Of course, floppy drive and controller card advertisements are neither standard nor complete. One ad might advertise "3.5 inch" while another might just say "1.44MB." In both cases, this means that the floppy disk drive uses 3.5-inch floppy disks.

Sometimes ads can be deceptive because they don't tell you everything the floppy disk drive or controller card has to offer. When an ad says that the controller card is an "HD/FD controller," this means that the controller card can control both hard disk and floppy disk drives, but you don't know how many hard disks and floppy disks it can control. Most controller cards can control up to two hard disks and two floppy disks, but a few can control two hard disks and four floppy disks.

When shopping for a floppy disk drives and controller cards, ask your dealer to answer any questions the ads might not tell you. To help you shop for a floppy disk drives and controller cards, use the following checklist as a guideline.

Floppy disk drive shopping checklist

**Type of 5.25-inch
floppy disk drives:**

❏ 1.2 MB   Price: _____

❏ 360K   Price: _____

**Type of 3.5-inch
floppy disk drives:**

❏ 21MB   Price: _____

❏ 2.88MB   Price: _____

❏ 1.44MB   Price: _____

❏ 720K   Price: _____

Controller card: ❑ Dedicated floppy drive controller card   Price: _____
                           ❑ Combination hard/floppy drive controller card Price: _____
                           ❑ Motherboard built-in controller card   Price: FREE

Controller card bus type: ❑ PCI   ❑ VESA
                                   ❑ EISA   ❑ ISA

Controller card I/O ports: ❑ Serial ports   ❑ Parallel ports
                                 ❑ None

Warranty: ❑ 3 Year   ❑ 2 Year
                 ❑ 1 Year   ❑ 30 Days

Dealer: _____

Price: _____

    The following section lists various "green" disk drives and disk drive controller cards. Most of these manufacturers will sell parts directly to individuals, or they can refer you to local or mail-order distributors.

"Green" disk drive manufacturers

3.5-inch Micro Floppy Disk Drive   Green Rating: *
Combination 1.2 inch/3.5 inch   (One star for energy conserving features)

Floppy Disk Drive
Teac Corporation
7733 Telegraph Road
Montebello, CA 90640
Tel: (213) 726-0303
Fax: (213) 727-7652
Comments: Teac also sells a 3.5-inch floppy disk drive called the FD-05HF/HFL, which consumes only 1.15 watts of power.

"Green" disk drive controller card manufacturers

Anti-Virus Multi-I/O Card   Green Rating: *
Silicon Star International, Inc.   (One star for energy conserving features)
47889 Fremont Blvd.
Fremont, CA 94538
Tel: (510) 623-0500
Fax: (510) 623-1092

Comments: This expansion card plugs into a VESA local bus slot and includes one floppy drive controller, one parallel port, two serial ports, and one game port. In addition, this card comes with a hardware-based anti-virus program to provide superior protection against boot-sector viruses. After a certain amount of keyboard or mouse inactivity, this controller will reduce the amount of power sent to the floppy disk drive.

4
Hard disk drives

The ideal "green" hard disk would consume little power and be small enough to require fewer materials to make than competing types of hard disks. When shopping for a hard disk, look for those that use a smaller platter size. The smaller the platter, the less material required to make it and the less power it will require.

Every computer needs a hard disk these days. Without a hard disk, your computer would be next to useless. Besides storing programs, hard disks also let you store massive amounts of your own data, such as word processor documents, spreadsheet files, and graphic images. As more programs gobble up several megabytes of disk space, the size of your hard disk can limit the capabilities of your computer.

Hard disk sizes and speeds

The amount of data that a hard disk can hold is measured in megabytes (abbreviated as MB) or gigabytes (abbreviated as GB). Ideally you should buy the largest hard disk you can afford because the longer you keep your computer, the more programs and files you'll need to store. Eventually you'll swamp a smaller hard disk and have to buy a second or replacement hard disk altogether. Hard disk sizes range from 130MB all the way up to 1.2GB.

In the curious world of hard disks, spending less often costs you more. For example, a 130MB hard disk might cost $170, or $1.31 per megabyte. Yet a 340MB hard disk might cost $275, or $0.81 per megabyte. Generally, the larger the hard disk, the less expensive per megabyte it will be. (Of course, you can get carried away and buy a huge hard disk and bankrupt yourself in the process.)

The hard disk size you need depends on what you plan to use your computer for. Word processor and spreadsheet files tend to be fairly small, database files slightly larger, and desktop publishing and graphic images largest of all. To make matters more confusing, the latest programs require several megabytes of storage. Microsoft Windows gobbles up 4MB of hard disk space, and Windows-based programs tend to require anywhere between 5MB to 75MB of storage space, depending on the specific application.

At the very least, don't look at any hard disk less than 200MB. For most people, a hard disk between 200MB and 400MB should be sufficient. Unless you're working with graphics, video, sound, or networks, you probably don't need all the storage space that a 1.2GB hard drive can offer.

Besides checking the size, check the access speed of any hard disk you buy. The access speed determines how fast the hard disk can retrieve data, and is measured in milliseconds (ms) like 12ms, 14ms, and 16ms. The higher the access speed, the slower the hard disk will be.

Controller cards

To work with a computer, a hard drive needs a controller card. This may be built into the motherboard or, more commonly, combined with a floppy drive controller on a single card. Some hard disks come with controller cards, while others do not. Most controller cards can support up to two hard disks.

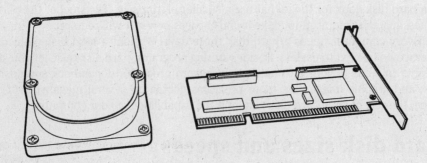

4-1 A hard disk and controller card.

Unfortunately, not all controller cards work with all types of hard disks. The two types of controller cards available follow one of two standards:

- IDE (integrated device electronics)
- SCSI (small computer system interface)

Most computers use IDE hard drives because they're less expensive and more popular. A typical IDE hard drive can transfer data at a rate of 4MB per second. However, for larger hard disks (ranging from 1.2GB to 2.4GB) the SCSI standard is used more often because it can transfer data at up to 10MB per second.

The controller card standard (IDE or SCSI) is less important than the type of expansion slot the controller card plugs in to. A hard disk controller card plugged into a VESA local bus will be faster than a similar controller card plugged into a slower ISA expansion bus. Table 4-1 lists the types of expansion slots a hard disk controller card can plug into, with the fastest and more efficient bus at the top and the slowest at the bottom.

**Table 4-1. Comparison of hard
drive controller standards and bus types**

Controller standard	Bus standard
SCSI	PCI
IDE	PCI
SCSI	VESA
IDE	VESA
SCSI	EISA
IDE	EISA
SCSI	ISA
IDE	ISA

When buying a hard disk, make sure that your controller card works with both your hard drive and your motherboard's expansion or local bus. To get your hard disk to work in your computer, you need to match up the hard drive controller card with:

- The right hard drive. (A hard drive that follows the IDE standard won't work with a controller card that follows the SCSI standard.)
- The right bus type. (A motherboard with an EISA expansion bus and a PCI local bus won't work with a controller card that needs to plug into a VESA bus.)

Drive bays

Internal hard drives mount in a drive bay inside the computer case (see Chapter 7 for more information on computer cases). The two possible drive bay sizes are 5.25 inch and 3.5 inch. A hard drive designed for a 3.5-inch drive bay can also be placed in a 5.25-inch drive bay; however, a hard drive designed for a 5.25-inch drive bay limits where you can install the hard drive. Generally, the smaller the hard drive, the easier it is to find space inside your computer to install it.

Hard cards

If you're willing to spend up to twice as much more for a hard disk but want one that's practically foolproof to install, then consider a unique combination hard disk/controller card called a "hard card."

A hard card plugs into an expansion slot in your computer (usually requiring an ISA or EISA bus). Once plugged in, the hard card is ready for use. Because of their convenience, many people prefer hard cards as a way of adding a second hard disk quickly and easily. Unfortunately, a typical 240MB hard card costs approximately $400, or $1.67 a megabyte. A typical 240MB internal hard drive only costs approximately $215, or $0.90 a megabyte.

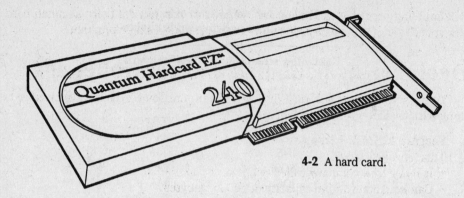

4-2 A hard card.

External hard disks

Although most hard disks sold these days are internal drives, some people prefer external drives. An external hard drives costs more and requires a separate electrical outlet to plug in, but then you'll have the advantage of being able to share hard disks between several computers.

Most external hard drives plug into a computer through the parallel port, making it easy to move the hard disk between a desktop and a laptop computer. Typical prices for an external hard disk costs $450 for a 130MB drive, or $3.46 per megabyte, which makes them the most expensive types of hard disks you can buy. Further, from a "green" point of view, neither hard cards nor external hard disks are practical because they cost more and require more materials to make. External hard disks are even worse because they must be plugged in, wasting more electricity than an internal hard disk.

Caches

In an effort to make hard disks even faster, some controller cards come with their own memory, called a hardware cache. Unfortunately, hardware caches tend to be expensive. As a cheaper alternative, many people buy a special program known as a software cache.

A software cache carves out a chunk of your computer's main memory, and sets this aside to store data that the computer will need next. While the computer is busy doing something else, the software cache yanks data off the hard disk and has it ready when the computer needs it.

Disk doublers

As a practical alternative to buying a large hard disk or a second hard disk, you can also buy a disk doubler program that compresses your files up to 50 percent of their original size, effectively doubling the size of your hard disk.

Such disk doubling programs cost much less than buying a second or larger hard disk, but they have their flaws. Some people have lost files after compressing their hard disk, while others have had their files scrambled. For most people, disk doubling programs have proven safe and reliable. After all, given that the cost for most disk doubling programs is $150 or less, where else can you get twice as much hard disk space without doing anything more than installing a single program?

Deciphering hard disk and controller ads

To help you shop for a hard disk drive, here are some typical advertisements along with their English translations:

Seagate 425MB, 13ms
This hard disk drive:
- Is made by a company called Seagate
- Can hold a maximum capacity of 425 megabytes
- Has an access speed of 13 milliseconds

340MB IDE
This hard disk drive:
- Can hold a maximum capacity of 340 megabytes
- Follows the IDE standard

EISA SCSI HD/FD controller
This controller card:
- Plugs into an EISA bus expansion slot
- Controls an SCSI hard drive
- Controls both hard disk and floppy disk drives

Super IDE 2HD/2FD 2S/1P/1G ports
This controller card:
- Works with IDE hard drives
- Controls up to two hard disk and two floppy disk drives
- Includes 2 serial ports, 1 parallel port, and 1 game port

Hard drive and controller card advertisements are rarely standard or complete. One ad might advertise "540MB" but not tell you whether the hard drive follows the IDE or SCSI standard. Another ad might describe a controller card as "IDE 2HD/2FD" but neglect to specify whether the controller card plugs into a VESA, EISA, or ISA bus.

When shopping for hard disk drives and controller cards, ask your dealer to answer any questions the ads might not tell you. To help you shop for a hard disk drives and controller cards, use the following checklist as a guideline.

Hard disk drive shopping checklist

Hard disk drive size: _____MB

Hard disk access speed: _____ms

Hard disk standard: ❑ IDE   ❑ SCSI

Controller card standard: ❑ IDE ❑ SCSI

Hardware cache on controller card: ❑ Yes ❑ No

Controller card bus required: ❑ PCI ❑ VESA
❑ EISA ❑ ISA

Controller card I/O ports: ❑ Serial ❑ Parallel
❑ Game ❑ None

Warranty: ❑ 3 Year ❑ 2 Year
❑ 1 Year ❑ 30 Days

Dealer:

_____

Price:

_____

5
Monitors

Of all the parts of a computer, the most dangerous and wasteful is the monitor. While the typical computer consumes 50 to 100 watts of electricity, the typical monitor consumes up to 250 watts of electricity.

Besides being energy hogs, monitors are the greatest source of electromagnetic radiation, which is suspected to cause cancer, cataracts, and leukemia. Whether or not scientists can prove a direct linkage between electromagnetic radiation and health problems remains debatable. But at the very least, poorly designed monitors are directly responsible for eye strain, headaches, and stiff neck muscles. In terms of cost, safety, and comfort, the most crucial part of any computer is its monitor.

The ideal "green" monitor should meet three criteria:
- Conserves energy
- Shields and protects a user from excessive electromagnetic radiation
- Displays crisp images, reduces glare, and adjusts easily for maximum comfort and convenience for the user

Energy Star

Before buying any monitor, look for the EPA Energy Star logo. To meet the Energy Star requirements, a monitor must be able to turn itself off if nobody touches the keyboard or mouse after a specified amount of time. During this "sleep" period, the power usage of the monitor must be no greater than 30 watts. When you buy an Energy Star monitor, you can be assured you're getting the minimum standard for a "green" monitor.

But some Energy Star monitors go a bit further than the Energy Star specification and provide three levels of power usage. At the first level, the monitor is being used and consumes a normal amount of power. At the second level, the monitor reduces power by 90% of its ordinary usage if the user doesn't touch the keyboard or mouse within a certain amount of time. The moment the user touches the keyboard or moves the mouse, the monitor returns to normal.

At the third and final level, the monitor shuts itself down after a prolonged period of inactivity, typically ranging from ten minutes to one hour. If the user doesn't touch the keyboard or move the mouse after this prolonged period, the monitor reduces power by up to 95% of its ordinary usage. The moment the user touches the keyboard or moves the mouse, the monitor may take several seconds to "warm up" and return to normal operation.

Be careful when choosing an Energy Star monitor. Some monitors (like the Nanao monitors) will automatically reduce power by themselves, regardless of the type of video adapter card you use. Other monitors will only reduce power when connected to a Display Power Management Signaling (DPMS) compliant video adapter card. If you buy a monitor that requires a DPMS-compliant video adapter card, but plug it into an ordinary video adapter card, the monitor may not reduce power to the Energy Star power requirements.

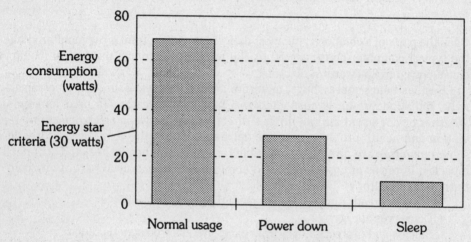

5-1 Graph showing power usage of a typical Energy Star monitor.

MPR II standards

To protect yourself from electromagnetic emissions, look for a monitor that meets the standard established by the Swedish National Board of Measurement and Testing in 1990, known by its Swedish initials as MPR. The latest MPR standard, dubbed MPR II, measures the strength of electrical and magnetic fields in two bands, at a half meter away. For you technical types out there, Band 1 falls between 5 Hz and 2 KHz and Band 2 falls between 2 KHz and 400 KHz.

In Band 1, electrical fields must be less than 25 volts per meter and magnetic fields must be less than 250 nanoteslas (2.5 milligauss). In Band 2, electrical fields must be less than 2.5 volts and magnetic fields must be less than 25 nanoteslas.

Basically, the MPR II standard restricts the amount of electromagnetic emissions that a monitor can release. Although some research suggests that even the MPR II standard may not be stringent enough (a more stringest Swedish emissions standard, called TCO, is an attempt to fix this problem), the less electromagnetic emissions the better. Given that monitors that meet the MPR II standard don't cost any more than those that don't, it only makes sense to buy an MPR II-compliant monitor for maximum safety.

FCC rating

Besides emitting electromagnetic fields, monitors may also release radio-frequency (RF) waves, which is the same electromagnetic radiation that radio and television sets receive. Although some studies suggest that prolonged exposure to radio-frequency waves have produced cataracts and changes in the blood chemistry, a more obvious problem involves interference to radio communications like radios, televisions, and cordless phones.

As an informal test, put a radio next to your monitor and turn the monitor on. If turning on the monitor causes static or distortion through the radio, then you'll know that the monitor is releasing excessive radio-frequency waves that are interfering with the radio receiver.

Besides messing up radio or television broadcasts, excessive radio-frequency waves have the more serious side effect of interfering with aircraft communications, emergency broadcast systems, and police frequencies. To identify equipment with reduced levels of radio-frequency waves, the Federal Communications Commission (FCC) certifies equipment with one of two FCC standards: Class A or Class B.

An FCC Class A rating is the weaker of the two ratings and certifies that equipment can be used in business offices. An FCC Class B rating certifies that equipment can be used in either a business or home. Because a home is more likely to have multiple televisions, radios, and cordless phones, a Class B-rated item is less likely to interfere than a Class A-rated item. Whenever possible, look for a monitor that has earned the FCC Class B rating. If a monitor has an FCC Class A rating or no rating at all, avoid it.

For your eyes only: reducing fuzziness

Besides the health hazards posed by electromagnetic emissions, monitors can also affect your health in more direct ways. The fuzzier the images displayed on the monitor, the more likely you'll suffer from eye strain, headaches, or dizziness. To avoid these problems, check a monitor's resolution, refresh rate, refresh method (interlace or noninterlace), and dot pitch.

Screen resolution

The resolution determines the number of dots a monitor uses to create images on the screen. The more dots used, the higher the resolution. Resolutions are measured horizontally and vertically, like 1280 (horizontally) by 1024 (vertically).

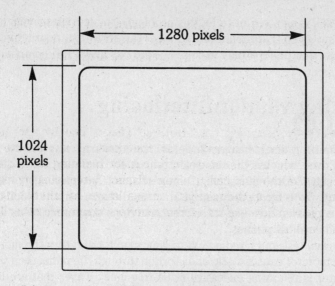

5-2 How screen resolution is measured.

The higher the resolution a monitor can display, the sharper its images can appear. However, the maximum resolution your monitor will display depends on the maximum resolution your video adapter card can produce. If you buy a cheap video adapter card and the most expensive monitor, you'll only see what the cheap video adapter card can produce. Likewise, if you buy an expensive video adapter card but a cheap monitor, you'll see only what the cheap monitor can display.

Refresh rate (bandwidth)

Even more important than the maximum resolution is the bandwidth or vertical refresh rate of the monitor. The refresh rate is measured in hertz (Hz) and refers to the speed at which the monitor constantly refreshes a displayed image. Monitors with low refresh rates tend to have a noticeable "flicker," causing eye strain or headaches in some people. Monitors with higher refresh rates exhibit less "flicker."

To eliminate "flickering" in monitors, the Video Electronics Standards Association (VESA) provides minimum refresh rate standards for different types of monitor resolutions. Table 5-1 lists the minimum refresh rate required to eliminate "flickering" for each resolution.

**Table 5-1. Monitor
resolution and bandwidth**

Video standard	Resolution	Bandwidth
VGA	640 × 480	72 Hz
SVGA	800 × 600	72 Hz
XGA	1024 × 768	70 Hz

Beware! Some monitors have a maximum resolution of 1024 by 768, but only a refresh rate of 50 Hz. If a monitor's refresh rate doesn't match the VESA standard, the monitor will appear to "flicker" and may contribute to eye irritation or dizziness.

Interlacing vs. noninterlacing

Monitors work by "scanning" or "drawing" images line by line across the screen. The refresh rate determines how fast the monitor scans an entire screen. However, monitors may use one of two methods for scanning an image. One is called interlacing; the other is called noninterlacing. Interlacing monitors scan every other line. To refresh the complete screen image, an interlacing monitor must make two passes. Because interlacing monitors skip every other line, they may cause additional "flickering."

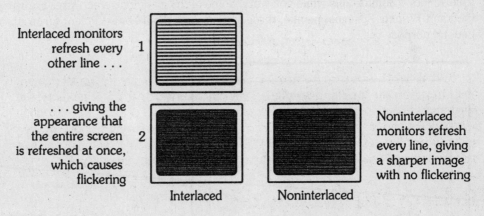

Interlaced monitors refresh every other line . . . 1

. . . giving the appearance that the entire screen is refreshed at once, which causes flickering 2

Noninterlaced monitors refresh every line, giving a sharper image with no flickering

Interlaced   Noninterlaced

5-3 How interlacing and noninterlacing work.

Noninterlacing means that the monitor scans every line. As a result, noninterlacing monitors have much less "flickering." Although interlacing monitors are usually less expensive, the price you pay in eye strain and headaches won't be worth it. Get a noninterlacing monitor instead.

Dot pitch

Another factor that determines the sharpness or fuzziness of a screen image on a monitor is the dot pitch. The dot pitch refers to the amount of space between each pixel displayed on the screen and is measured in millimeters (mm). The smaller the dot pitch, the sharper the image will look.

Dot pitches range from .51 mm down to .18 mm, although the most common dot pitches range between .26 mm and .22 mm. When looking for a monitor, make sure the dot pitch lies within this range. Naturally, the smaller the dot pitch, the more you will have to pay for the monitor.

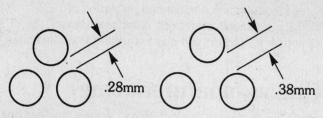

5-4 How dot pitch is measured.

Screen size and type

The size of a screen also determines the appearance of a monitor's image. Screens are measured diagonally in inches and range from 14 inch all the way up to 21 inch. Smaller monitors naturally cost less, but larger monitors let you display multiple windows comfortably while you work. Some of the common screen sizes are 15 inch and 17 inch. For most people, these screen sizes should be sufficient for most general purpose use.

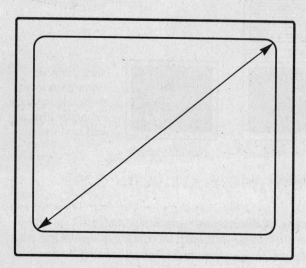

5-5 How screen sizes are measured.

Ergonomic factors

For maximum comfort, get a monitor that comes with a tilt and swivel base, which lets you adjust the angle of the monitor. As an alternative, you can buy a special monitor arm that holds the monitor in the air, letting you adjust both its angle and its height.

Recycled materials

Finally, check to see if a monitor is made from recycled plastics. Instead of building a monitor from recycled materials, some manufacturers simply use recycled pa-

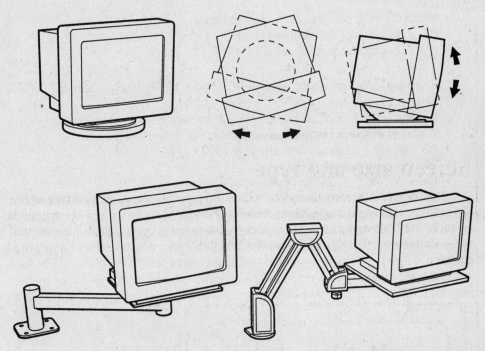

5-6 Tilt and swivel bases and monitor arms.

per to package the monitor. Others not only use recycled materials, but use materials that don't require chlorofluorocarbons (CFCs), which can leak into the atmosphere and destroy the ozone layer.

Deciphering monitor advertisements

To help you dig through the advertising claims for monitors, here are some typical monitor advertisements along with their English translations:

VGA 17" Monitor (1280 × 1024) Noninterlace .26dp
This monitor:
- Follows the old VGA standard of a minimum resolution of 640 × 480
- Has a diagonal screen size of 17 inches
- Has a maximum resolution of 1280 ×1024
- Uses noninterlacing for less "flickering"
- Has a dot pitch of .26 millimeters

Nanao, Energy Star, MPR-II, FCC B, .28 (1024 × 768)
This monitor:
- Is made by a company called Nanao
- Follows the EPA's Energy Star guidelines
- Follows the Swedish MPR-II low emission standard

- Meets the FCC standard for a Class B rating
- Has a dot pitch of .28 millimeters
- Has a maximum resolution of 1024 × 768

Low emissions, Power management, 1600 × 1200, 80 Hz, .26mm
This monitor:
- Is designed to reduce and shield users from electromagnetic radiation
- Contains a built-in feature to save and conserve electricity
- Can display a maximum resolution of 1600 × 1024
- Has a refresh rate of 80 Hz
- Has a dot pitch of .266 millimeters

Monitor ads either bombard you with too much technical information, or not enough. One ad might claim "low emissions," but this doesn't tell you whether it meets the MPR-II standard for low emissions. Another ad might claim "power management feature," but ignore any mention of whether it meets the EPA's Energy Star guidelines.

When shopping for a monitor, ask your dealer to answer any questions the ads might not tell you. To help you shop for the perfect "green" monitor, use the following checklist.

Monitor shopping checklist

Energy Star compliant: ❑ Yes   ❑ No

Requires a DPMS compliant video adapter card: ❑ Yes   ❑ No

MPR II compliant: ❑ Yes   ❑ No

FCC Class Rating: ❑ Class A   ❑ Class B
                                       ❑ None

Maximum Screen Resolution: ❑ 1280 × 1024   ❑ 1024 × 768
                                       ❑ 800 × 600   ❑ 640 × 480

Refresh Rate: ❑ Over 80 Hz   ❑ Between 80 Hz and 70 Hz
                                       ❑ Under 70 Hz

Interlacing/noninterlacing: ❑ Interlacing   ❑ Noninterlacing

Dot Pitch: ❑ Under .22mm   ❑ Between .22mm and .26mm
                                       ❑ Over .26mm

Screen size:
- ❏ 21-inch
- ❏ 17-inch
- ❏ 14-inch
- ❏ 20-inch
- ❏ 15-inch

Flat screen: ❏ Yes ❏ No

Antiglare coating: ❏ Yes ❏ No

Tilt and swivel base: ❏ Yes ❏ No

Made from recycled materials: ❏ Yes ❏ No

Warranty:
- ❏ 3 Year
- ❏ 1 Year
- ❏ 2 Year
- ❏ 30 Days

Dealer:

_____

Price:

_____

The following lists some companies that sell "green" monitors.

"Green" monitor manufacturers

ADI System, Inc.
2115 Ringwood Avenue
San Jose, CA 95131
Tel: (408) 944-0100
Fax: (408) 944-0300

Green Rating: **
(One star for Energy Star compliance)
(One star for MPR II compliance)

IBM
Building 203
3039 Cornwallis Road
Research Triangle Park
NC 27709
Tel: (800) 426-2968
Fax: (800) 426-4182

Green Rating: ***
(One star for Energy Star compliance)
(One star for MPR II compliance)
(One star for IBM's donations to fund
environmental research)

Idek
650 Louis Drive, #120
Warminster, PA 18974
Tel: (215) 957-6543
Fax: (215) 957-6551

Green Rating: **
(One star for Energy Star compliance)
(One star for MPR II compliance)

Kuo Feng Corp. (KFC)
1575 Sunflower Avenue
Costa Mesa, CA 92626
Tel: (714) 546-0336
Fax: (714) 546-0315

Green Rating: **
(One star for Energy Star compliance)
(One star for MPR II compliance)

MAG InnoVision, Inc.
2801 South Yale Street
Santa Ana, CA 92704
Tel: (714) 751-2008
Fax: (714) 751-5522

Green Rating: ***
(One star for Energy Star compliance)
(One star for MPR II compliance)
(One star for avoiding ozone depleting
materials during manufacturing and
packaging)

Mitsubishi Electronics America, Inc.
5665 Plaza Drive
P.O. Box 6007
Cypress, CA 90630-0007
Tel: (714) 236-4845

Green Rating: **
(One star for Energy Star compliance)
(One star for MPR II compliance)

Nanao Corporation
23535 Telo Avenue
Torrance, CA 90505
Tel: (310) 325-5202
Fax: (310) 530-1679

Green Rating: ***
(One star for Energy Star compliance)
(One star for MPR II compliance)
(One star for using recycled containers
that only use soy ink)

Optiquest
20490 Business Parkway
Walnut, CA 91789
Tel: (909) 468-3750
Fax: (909) 468-3770

Green Rating: **
(One star for Energy Star compliance)
(One star for MPR II compliance)

Proview Electronics Corporation
6200 Savoy Drive, Suite 510
Houston, TX 77036
Tel: (713) 784-6632
Fax: (714) 784-7390

Green Rating: **
(One star for Energy Star compliance)
(One star for MPR II compliance)

Sony Electronics
3300 Zanker Road
San Jose, CA 95134
Tel: (408) 432-0190

Green Rating: ***
(One star for Energy Star compliance)
(One star for MPR II compliance)
(One star for being made from ozone-
friendly materials and packed in a
recyclable container)

Samtron
14251 E. Firestone Blvd.
Suite 101
La Mirada, CA 90638
Tel: (310) 802-8425
Fax: (310) 802-8820

Green Rating: ***
(One star for Energy Star compliance)
(One star for MPR II compliance)
(One star for using recycled containers)

Samsung Electronics
105 Challenger Road
Ridgefield Park, NJ 07660
Tel: (201) 229-4132
Fax: (201) 229-4029

Green Rating: **
(One star for Energy Star compliance)
(One star for MPR II compliance)

Tatung Company
2850 El Presidio Street
Long Beach, CA 90810
Tel: (310) 637-2105

Green Rating: **
(One star for Energy Star compliance)
(One star for MPR II compliance)

ViewSonic
20480 Business Parkway
Walnut CA 91789
Tel: (909) 869-7976
Fax: (909) 869-7318

Green Rating: **
(One star for Energy Star compliance)
(One star for MPR II compliance)

Zenith Data Systems
2150 East Lake Cook Road
Buffalo Grove, IL 60089
Tel: (800) 952-3099
Fax: (800) 472-7211
BBS: (708) 808-2264

Green Rating: **
(One star for Energy Star compliance)
(One star for MPR II compliance)

6
Video adapter cards

Even the best monitor in the world is worthless without a video adapter card. Video adapter cards plug into an expansion slot in your computer and control the appearance of the images on your monitor screen.

Two of the most important factors in choosing a video adapter card are its speed and display capabilities. The faster your video adapter card is, the more responsive your monitor will appear in displaying graphics or animation. The higher the display capabilities of the video adapter card, the sharper the images and the more colors your monitor can display. As graphical user interfaces (like Microsoft Windows and OS/2), multimedia, and video editing become commonplace, a fast, high-quality video adapter card will be a necessity for any computer.

"Green" video adapter cards

Look for video adapter cards that follow the VESA DPMS standard, which lets the video card reduce power to DPMS-compliant monitors. If your monitor has the ability to turn itself off (like the Nanao monitor), then you won't need such a "green" video adapter card.

Bus type

Your monitor plugs into a video adapter card, which in turn plugs into an expansion slot in your computer. However, different video adapter cards plug into different expansion slots. The four types of expansion slots that video adapter cards can plug into are:

- PCI local bus   (Fastest)
- VESA local bus
- EISA
- ISA   (Slowest)

Because the bus type determines the speed that data can move between the computer and the video adapter card, video adapter cards designed for ISA and

EISA expansion slots will be fine for normal use, but too slow for graphics-intensive work like CAD, animation, or desktop video. If you need fast, colorful graphics, your first investment should be a motherboard with a VESA or PCI local bus.

Resolution and color

Besides making sure that your video adapter card fits in your computer's expansion slots, you also have to make sure that your video adapter card's resolution matches your monitor's resolution. If the two resolutions don't match, then your monitor may not work with your video adapter card.

To maintain compatibility with a wide range of monitors, most video adapter cards can display at several levels of resolution:

- 1280×1024
- 1024×768
- 800×600
- 640×480

The higher the resolution, the fewer the colors the video adapter card can display. For example, most video adapter cards can display up to 16 million colors (of course, how many people can actually recognize that many colors is another question altogether) at 640×480 resolution, but at 1280×1024 resolution, the video adapter card may only display 16 colors.

To display more colors at higher resolutions, a video adapter card needs the fastest bus possible (PCI or VESA), plus lots of memory of its own.

Memory

The amount of memory that a video adapter card contains can be 256K, 512K, 1MB, 2MB, 3MB, 4MB, and even 5MB. The more memory, the more colors the video adapter card can display at higher resolutions. For example, a 1MB video adapter card might only display 16 colors at a resolution of 1024×768, but a video adapter card with 4MB might display 16.7 million colors at that same resolution.

Besides the amount of memory, the speed and type of the memory chips can affect the video adapter card's performance. Some video adapter cards use memory chips that run at 70 nanoseconds (ns) while others use the faster and more expensive 60ns chips. For additional speed, the faster video adapter cards use Video RAM (VRAM) chips instead of the slower Dynamic RAM (DRAM) chips. VRAM can send information to the screen while simultaneously loading more information in memory. As a result, video adapter cards with VRAM work much faster. If speed is essential, look for VRAM memory chips.

Software drivers

For people who need fast graphics and use a well-known program like AutoCAD, WordPerfect, or Microsoft Windows, some video adapter cards come with software drivers. These drivers optimize certain programs for displaying graphics with that particular video adapter card. If you don't use a popular program, your video adapter card probably won't have a software driver for you.

Ports

Although ports have nothing to do with the quality of your video images, many video adapter cards come with built-in serial or parallel ports, just to add extra value and save an expansion slot in your computer.

If you already have enough ports built into your motherboard or built into your hard drive/floppy drive controller, then you can save money by avoiding video adapter cards with built-in ports.

Deciphering video adapter card advertisements

When shopping for a video adapter card, it's usually a good idea to buy it from the same place where you bought your monitor. That way your dealer can tell you whether the monitor and the video adapter card will work together. (And if they don't, then you only have one dealer to complain to.)

To help you wade through the technical descriptions in video adapter advertisements, the following are sample magazine ads, translated into plain English.

Cirrus logic VLB w/1MB
This video adapter card:
- Is made by a company called Cirrus Logic
- Plugs into a VESA local bus expansion slot
- Comes with 1MB of memory

Viper VLB 2MB VRAM
This video adapter card:
- Is called the Viper
- Plugs into a VESA local bus expansion slot
- Comes with 2MB of memory, using the faster VRAM memory chips

Super VGA 1024 × 768 w/1MB
This video adapter card:
- Can display a maximum resolution of 1024 × 768
- Comes with 1MB of memory

Like most advertisements for computer parts, some ads leave out more information than they give you. For example, some ads specifically mention "VLB" to let you know they plug into a VESA local bus expansion slot. However, some ads won't mention the bus type at all. It could plug into a ISA, EISA, VESA, or PCI expansion slot. From the ad alone, it's impossible to tell.

To help you find the right video adapter card for your computer, use the following checklist:

Video adapter card checklist

DPMS compliant: ❏ Yes ❏ No

Bus type required: ❏ PCI ❏ VESA
  ❏ EISA ❏ ISA

Maximum resolution: ❏ 1280 × 1024 ❏ 1024 × 768
  ❏ 800 × 600 ❏ 640 × 480

Included memory: ❏ 5MB ❏ 4MB
  ❏ 3MB ❏ 2MB
  ❏ 1MB ❏ 512K
  ❏ 256K ❏ None

Ports: ❏ Serial ❏ Parallel
  ❏ None

Warranty: ❏ 3 Year ❏ 2 Year
  ❏ 1 Year ❏ 30 Days

Dealer:

_____

Price:

_____

The following manufacturer sells a video adapter card that offers low power consumption features:

Optiquest
20490 Business Parkway
Walnut, CA 91789
Tel: (909) 468-3750
Fax: (909) 468-3770

Comments: Optiquest sells a DPMS compliant video adapter card with a built-in parallel port. When a noncompliant DPMS monitor and printer is plugged into the video adapter card, the card will power down both the monitor and printer when the computer is not in use.

7

Cases and power supplies

Everything fits inside the case, so make sure you get the type of case that meets your needs. Ideally, you want a case that takes up the least amount of space on your desk, but offers the maximum amount of space inside for adding expansion cards in the future. No matter what the capabilities of your motherboard may be, the type of case you buy may limit the capabilities of your computer.

Types of cases

Cases come in one of five sizes:
- Towers
- Mini-towers
- Desktop
- Small-footprint
- Slimline

Tower cases are usually too large for ordinary use. Unless you're someone who absolutely needs as many computer accessories as possible stuffed into a single computer case, you can save your money and avoid tower cases. Most people use tower cases in networks for file servers, because there's plenty of room for expansion inside.

Mini-tower cases are a little more than one and a half feet high, making them perfect for tucking under a desk or pushing to one side of your desk. Because of their compact size, mini-tower cases are more likely to have one or more four-inch-wide drive bays, suitable only for 3.5-inch floppy disk drives. When considering a mini-tower, make sure it has enough drive bays of the right size for the hard drive, floppy drive, CD-ROM drive, and tape backup units you may want to install.

Desktop cases are the most common. Some people flip a desktop case on its side and stuff the whole thing under their desk, but most people put a desktop case directly on top of their desk (hence the name desktop case). Desktop cases are useful when you need easy access to floppy, CD-ROM, or tape drives and don't feel like bending underneath your desk to reach them.

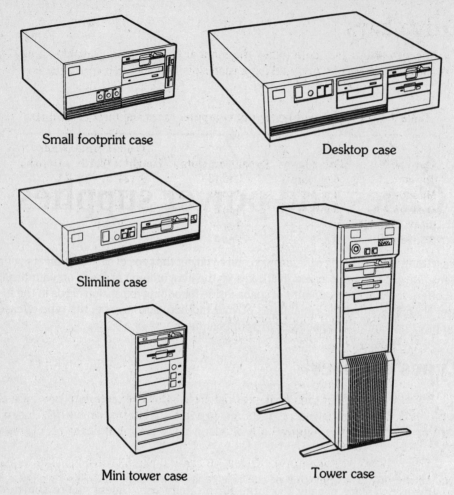

Small footprint case

Desktop case

Slimline case

Mini tower case

Tower case

7-1 Different types of cases available.

Small-footprint cases are narrower than desktop cases, limit the number of drive bays and expansion slots available, but take up less space on your desk. If saving a few inches is worth losing one or two drive bays or expansion slots, then consider a small-footprint case.

Slimline cases are smaller in width and height (as if people have trouble reaching over the top of their computer at times). A slimline case limits the number of drive bays and expansion slots available, because of its minuscule size. The cramped size of a slimline case also introduces the possibility of overheating, especially if you're using a fast processor like a 486 or Pentium.

If you are absolutely sure that you'll never want to expand the capabilities of your computer anytime between now and the next century, get a slimline case. Otherwise, spend a little more money and get a desktop or mini-tower case instead.

Drive bays

The size of the case determines the number of drive bays available. Table 7-1 lists the number of drive bays and expansion slots found in each type of case.

Table 7-1. Comparison of different computer cases and their capabilities

Case type	Drive bays	Expansion slots	Typical dimensions (Height × Width × Depth)
Tower	6 or more	8 to 12	24" × 6" × 17"
Mini-tower	4 or 5	6 to 8	17" × 6" × 17"
Desktop	3 to 5	4 to 6	6" × 21" × 17"
Small-footprint	3 or 4	4 or 5	6" × 16" × 16"
Slimline	2 or 3	2 to 4	4" × 16" × 16"

Each drive bay can hold one of the following:
- One 5.25-inch or 3.5-inch floppy drive
- One combo 5.25-inch/3.5-inch floppy drive
- One hard drive
- One tape backup drive
- One CD-ROM drive

You can buy both internal and external drives. However, internal drives are always less expensive than external drives. In addition, internal drives don't need a case or external power supply, both of which are wasteful in terms of a "green" PC.

If you choose to use internal drives, be careful! Not all drive bays are equal. Due to the physical limitation of the case, drive bays come in different sizes and types:
- Six-inch-wide drive bays (sometimes called 5.25-inch drive slots)
- Four-inch-wide drive bays (sometimes called 3.5-inch drive slots)
- Accessible from the outside of the case
- Inaccessible from outside the case

A six-inch-wide drive bay gives you the option of installing different-sized units, like a 5.25-inch floppy disk drive or a smaller 3.5-inch floppy disk drive. A four-inch-wide drive bay limits you to smaller units, like a 3.5-inch floppy disk drive.

Not all drive bays may be accessible from the outside. Sometimes the case will cover one or more drive bays, making them inaccessible from the outside. Inaccessible drive bays are used for hard drives, because you never need access to them. Accessible drive bays are used for floppy disk drives, CD-ROM, and tape backup units. The more six-inch-wide, accessible drive bays a case offers, the greater your options will be for adding additional drives later.

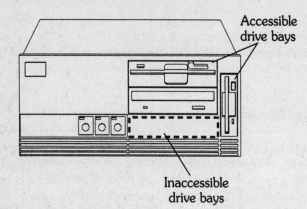

7-2 Typical accessible/ inaccessible drive bays in a computer case.

Expansion slots

Your motherboard determines the number of expansion slots available, but your case determines how many of those expansion slots are accessible from the back. Some cases cover one or two expansion slots, which may be fine for plugging in a disk drive controller card; but if you need to add a serial or parallel port, then you wouldn't want to plug it into a covered expansion slot.

Generally, you won't have to worry about covered expansion slots, because you can always find enough expansion cards that don't need to be accessed from the back (drive controller cards, for example). Just remember that the more expansion slots there are that open from the back, the greater your expansion possibilities will be.

Material

Most cases are made out of a combination of plastic and metal, or just metal. The quality of plastic cases can vary drastically. Some plastic cases are tough enough to withstand a few kicks and bangs. Other plastic cases feel weak and flimsy, almost as if putting a monitor on top of them will crush them in an instant.

To provide shielding against electromagnetic emissions and radio-frequency waves, as well as strengthening the case, plastic cases come with metal sheets or frames. For the ultimate in durability, cost, and shielding, you can buy all-metal cases. Whether a case is made from steel, or plastic reinforced with a metal frame, make sure it meets the FCC Class B rating for shielding electromagnetic emissions.

Although metal cases may be more durable, plastic cases have the advantage of being recyclable. Note that recyclable plastic is often virgin plastic that simply has a rating that identifies the type of plastic used, but recycled plastic is made from previously used plastic.

A plastic rating, developed by the plastic industry's Partnership for Plastics Progress, identifies the type of plastic resin that has been used. This rating makes it easy to sort plastics for later recycling. The "greenest" plastic cases consist of recycled plastics plus a plastics rating for easy recycling later.

Finally, most cases come apart easily by removing several screws, but some cases snap apart or have oversize screws that you can loosen and tighten with your fingers. Obviously the more convenient the case is to take apart, the less trouble it will be to upgrade your computer at a later date.

Power supply

The power supply supplies electricity to the computer and keeps the computer cool with a cooling fan. Power supplies are designed to fit into specific types of cases, so a power supply designed for a tower case will be too big to fit into a slimline case.

Usually it's more convenient to buy a computer case and a power supply together so you know the two will fit. But it's perfectly all right to buy them separately as long as you take care to measure the computer case and the power supply's dimensions so they will fit together.

Once you get the right size power supply, look at the wattage rating. The higher the wattage, the more peripherals and expansion cards the computer can handle, but also the more electricity the power supply consumes. Wattage ratings range from 60 watts all the way up to 300 watts or higher.

Some "green" PCs use a 60-watt power supply, which consumes less electricity (and thus may be more efficient from a "green" point of view) but also limits future expansion. If you add too many expansion cards into a computer with a weak power supply, you could overload the power supply and the additional expansion cards won't work. Some of the newest "green" power supplies can power down the computer and the monitor (if the monitor is plugged into the computer and not in a separate outlet).

If you don't plan to plug in expansion cards any time soon, a lower wattage power supply should be sufficient as well as saving you a little extra in electricity costs. If you want to leave room for future expansion, make sure you get a heftier power supply, such as a 200-watt power supply or better.

Besides supplying electricity, power supplies also provide a fan to keep the inside of the computer cool. In hot climates or during hot days, it's possible for your computer to overheat, especially if you're using a fast 80486DX or Pentium processor. (You can actually burn your fingertip by touching the processor while the computer is running; don't try this on a regular basis!)

Many power supply fans sound like Boeing 747s revving up for takeoff, but the latest power supplies have extra-quiet fans. Because any additional noise will likely grate on your nerves after a while, look for power supplies with ultra-quiet or noise-reduced fans. If you get a low-wattage power supply, you may not need a fan at all.

As an additional bonus, many power supplies may offer "overload protection," which protects your computer against power surges. If a power surge hits your computer, it could fry every electrical part inside it. Although this occurrence happens rarely, many power supplies provide overload protection just in case.

With these power supplies, the power supply (rather than the computer) gets fried by a damaging power surge, much like an overzealous Secret Service man diving in front of an assassin's bullet to protect the President. For additional safety, a power supply with overload protection can be worth buying.

Uninterruptable power supplies (UPS)

For an extra cost, you can buy an emergency power supply that contains its own batteries. The moment you lose electricity, the UPS unit keeps your computer files alive by immediately supplying the computer with electricity stored in its batteries. With a UPS, you can ensure that you will never lose any work because of a power outage.

If you absolutely must keep your computer running at all times, a UPS can be a sound investment. For most people, a UPS represents a luxury that you may not ever need. If you're spending most of your time playing computer games, then losing your high score may be inconvenient but certainly not catastrophic.

Control panels

To make it easy to control your computer, many cases offer a control panel that includes a keylock, on/off button, turbo button, a reset button, and a power down button.

The key lock lets you physically prevent anyone from using your computer. The only way to defeat a locked computer is to rip the case apart. Of course, if you lose your key you can't use your computer either, and you'll have to have a spare key made. If you're concerned that people may use your computer when you're not around, a case with a lock can offer a minimum level of security.

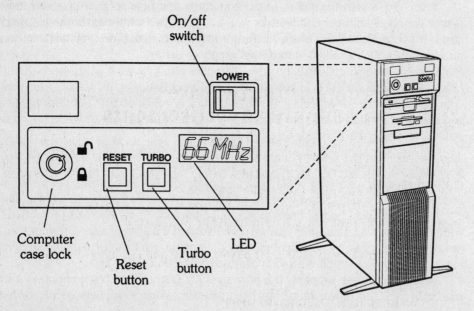

7-3 A typical control panel.

Many cases also include an digital display that shows how fast the computer is running at a given time, like 33 MHz or 50 MHz. With a turbo button, you can adjust the speed of your computer, which may be necessary because some programs don't work as well at high speeds. (Try playing Pac-Man at 66 MHz and the computer will wipe you out before you have a chance to move.)

Such displays are certainly convenient, although far from necessary. Because the cost of a case with a digital display isn't much greater than a case without a digital display, your decision will be based more on aesthetic reasons than anything else.

The reset button, on the other hand, is more important. Sometimes if your computer crashes or "hangs up," the only way to fix the problem is to start your computer all over again. If you turn the computer off and then on again, that's known as a "cold boot." If you press the Ctrl-Alt-Del keys, that's known as a "warm boot" because the computer is still on.

Cold boots are used when nothing else works. They always work, but turning your computer off and then on again causes a minor power surge to rush through your computer's circuits. Doing this too often could potentially damage your computer in the long run.

A keyboard warm boot (pressing Ctrl-Alt-Del) is much easier on your computer's circuits, because the power is never turned off. Unfortunately, some programs can crash your computer and your keyboard, rendering your keyboard absolutely useless. In these cases, pressing the Ctrl-Alt-Del keys won't do a thing. Instead, you have to press the computer's reset button to cause a warm boot.

Like a cold boot, a reset button's warm boot always works, but like a warm boot, it isn't as harsh on your computer's circuits. Because of this, it's a good idea to have a reset button in a computer case.

Many "green" computer cases also offer a power down button. Pressing this button immediately reduces power to the computer and monitor. Such a power down button can be useful when you know you're leaving your computer for an extended period of time. Rather than wait for the computer to reduce power by itself, you can reduce its electricity consumption right away.

Deciphering computer case and power supply advertisements

Many computer cases come priced with a power supply. Other times you have to buy the case and the power supply separately. When shopping for a computer case and power supply, it's usually a good idea to buy from the same place, so the dealer can find the right size power supply for your case.

To acquaint you with different case and power supply advertisements, the following are sample magazine ads, translated into plain English.

Full-size tower with 200-watt power supply and ten bays
This case:
- Is a tower case
- Comes with a 200-watt power supply
- Has ten drive bays

Low-profile case with two exposed 5.25", one exposed 3.5", and one internal 5.25" drive slots

This case:

- Is a slimline case
- Has four drive bays total, one of which is inaccessible from the user
- Has three of the larger drive bays and one of the smaller drive bays

Desktop Baby AT × 4 Bays, 200 watt, digital

This case:

- Is either a small footprint or desktop case
- Comes with four drive bays
- Comes with a 200-watt power supply
- Has a digital display

AT230W 6" × 8.5" × 6" UL

This power supply:

- Is designed to fit into AT style cases, like desktop or small footprint cases
- Is a 230-watt power supply
- Measures 6 inches by 8.5 inches by 6 inches
- Has passed tests conducted by the Underwriter's Laboratory (UL)

270W Silencer

This power supply:

- Is a 270-watt power supply
- Has a name of "Silencer," implying that the power supply has a quiet cooling fan

Advertisements for cases and power supplies are notorious for being incomplete. For example, some ads describe a case as being "AT style." Unfortunately, "AT style" can mean different things to different people. Sometimes an "AT style" case means a desktop case and sometimes it means a small footprint case. When in doubt, ask for the exact dimensions of the case before ordering.

To help you find the right case and power supply for your computer, use the following checklist:

Case and power supply checklist

Case type:
- ❑ Tower
- ❑ Desktop
- ❑ Slimline
- ❑ Mini-tower
- ❑ Small footprint

Total number of drive bays:

_____

Number that are accessible:

_____

Number of six-inch-wide drive bays:

_____

Number of four-inch-wide drive bays:

_____

Number of expansion slots exposed in the back:

_____

Case material: ❏ Plastic/metal   ❏ Metal
                      ❏ Recycled or recyclable plastic and metal

Key lock: ❏ Yes   ❏ No

Digital display: ❏ Yes   ❏ No

Turbo button: ❏ Yes   ❏ No

Reset button: ❏ Yes   ❏ No

Power down button: ❏ Yes   ❏ No

Power supply wattage:

_____

Overload protection: ❏ Yes   ❏ No

Quiet Cooling Fan: ❏ Yes   ❏ No

Warranty: ❏ 3 Year   ❏ 2 Year
                     ❏ 1 Year   ❏ 30 Days

Dealer:
_____

Price:

_____

   The following lists "green" cases and power supplies manufacturers and distributors. "Green" cases are those made from recycled plastics. "Green" power supplies automatically reduce electricity to the computer and monitor after a certain period of inactivity. In addition, "green" power supplies use low amounts of electricity, often eliminating the need for cooling fans.

"Green" computer case manufacturers

Palo Alto Design Group   Green Rating: *
360 University Avenue   (One star for using recycled plastics)
Palo Alto, CA 94301
Tel: (415) 617-9623

United Solutions, Inc.   Green Rating: *
6382 Arizona Circle   (One star for using recycled plastics)
Los Angeles, CA 90045
Tel: (310) 645-3232
Fax: (310) 645-0044

"Green" power supply manufacturers

Antron Technologies, Inc.   Green Rating: *
268 East Arrow Highway   (One star for energy-conserving features)
San Dimas, CA 91773
Tel: (909) 394-4522
Fax: (909) 394-1341

Astec Standard Power   Green Rating: *
401 Jones Road   (One star for energy-conserving features)
Oceanside, CA 92054
Tel: (619) 757-1880
Fax: (619) 439-4243

Exide Electronics   Green Rating: *
8521 Six Forks Road   (One star for energy-conserving features)
Raleigh, NC 27615
Tel: (919) 872-3020
Fax: (919) 870-3300

Key Power Inc.   Green Rating: *
11853 E. Telegraph Road   (One star for energy-conserving features)
Santa Fe Springs, CA 90670
Tel: (310) 948-2084
Fax: (310) 942-0536

Mecer Corporation   Green Rating: *
29560 Union City Blvd.   (One star for energy-conserving features)
Union City, CA 94587
Tel: (510) 476-5730
Fax: (510) 475-0982

Optiquest, Inc.   Green Rating: *
20490 Business Parkway   (One star for energy-conserving features)
Walnut, CA 91789
Tel: (909) 468-3750

Pao-Ku International   Green Rating: *
1053 Shore Road   (One star for energy-conserving features)
Naperville, IL 60563
Tel: (708) 369-5199
Fax: (708) 369-6068

PC&C Research Corp.
1100 Avenida Acaso
Camarillo, CA 93012
Tel: (805) 484-1685
Fax: (805) 987-8088

Green Rating: *
(One star for energy-conserving features)

Comments: PC&C Research sells a special power supply called the DataSaver, which stores all data and programs in memory onto the hard disk. When you turn off the computer, the DataSaver saves your work to the hard disk. When you turn the computer back on, the DataSaver restores your program exactly as it looked when you turned the computer off.

Senstron Electronic
268 East Arrow Highway
San Dimas, CA 91773
Tel: (909) 394-4522
Fax: (909) 394-1341

Green Rating: *
(One star for energy-conserving features)

United Solutions, Inc.
6382 Arizona Circle
Los Angeles, CA 90045
Tel: (310) 645-3232
Fax: (310) 645-0044

Green Rating: *
(One star for energy-conserving features)

8
Ports

Ports are nothing more than holes in the back of your computer that let you plug in extra peripherals, like a printer, modem, scanner, joystick, or external tape backup unit. The five most common types of ports a computer needs are:
- Serial ports (sometimes called RS-232 ports)
- Parallel ports (sometimes called printer or Centronics ports)
- Game ports (sometimes called joystick ports)
- SCSI ports (sometimes called SCSI-2 ports)
- Network ports

Because every computer needs ports, how do you add them to your computer? Generally, there are three places where a port may appear:
- Built into the motherboard
- On a separate expansion card, one or two ports per card
- On a multifunction expansion card that combines one or two ports along with other functions, like a clock/calendar, modem, extra memory, floppy/hard disk controller, etc.

Serial ports (RS-232 ports)

Serial ports come in two sizes (25 pin and 9 pin) and two sexes (male or female). Most computers have at least one serial port although you can add up to four serial ports. Programs identify serial ports in your computer as COM1 (for the first serial port), COM2 (for the second serial port), and so on.

Some of the most common items to connect to a serial port are:
- A mouse
- An external modem
- Printers
- Networks

Always make sure you get the right cables to plug into your serial port. If you get a cable that won't plug into your serial port, you can buy a device called a "gender bender," which plugs into your serial port.

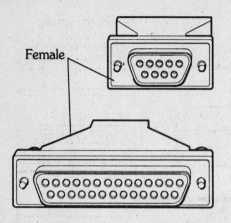
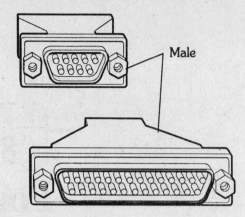

Female

Male

8-1 Different sizes and sexes of serial ports.

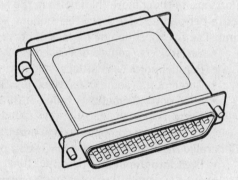

8-2 Different types of gender benders.

Parallel ports (printer or Centronics ports)

Parallel ports are often called printer ports because the most common peripheral connected to them are printers. Sometimes parallel ports may be referred to as Centronics ports, because they were originally used to connect to printers made by a company called Centronics.

Most computers have one parallel port, usually identified as LPT1 (for the first parallel port), LPT2 (for the second parallel port) and so on. Sometimes parallel ports may be referred to as PRN devices. Instead of adding a second parallel port, many people add a switch box, which lets two or more devices connect to a single parallel port.

The latest high-speed modems now use parallel ports instead of serial ports for added speed and reliability. These modems run at speeds up to 28,800 bps and follow the V.Fast Class (V.FC) standard for telecommunications. If you buy one of these high-speed modems, make sure you have a parallel port to plug it into.

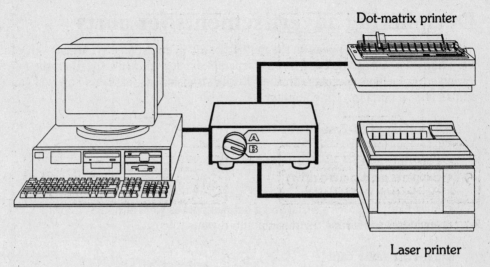

Dot-matrix printer

Laser printer

8-3 A typical switch box arrangement

Game ports

The most common items that plug into game ports are joysticks for playing games. Game ports are almost always found on separate expansion cards or on multifunction expansion cards. Some expansion cards only provide one game port, while others offer two or more.

If you don't plan on playing games that require a joystick, you can save money by leaving out a game port. However, if you want the ultimate in realism while playing your latest flight simulation game, then a game port will be worth the small amount (approximately $20) that it costs.

SCSI ports

SCSI ports are often used for large-capacity external hard disks (usually 540MB or more), tape backup units, or CD-ROM drives. Most computers don't have a SCSI port because SCSI devices are relatively uncommon.

The greatest advantage of an SCSI port is that it lets you connect up to seven SCSI devices in a line or "daisy-chain." Anytime you need to add a new SCSI device, you can plug it into the last one. The disadvantage of SCSI ports is that more available storage devices (hard disks, tape drive units) follow the IDE standard.

Network ports

For simplicity, many small networks connect through a computer's serial port. However, for greater efficiency, the larger networks require a separate network port. Network ports are always found on separate expansion cards.

Deciphering advertisements for ports

Because ports can appear on the motherboard, on an expansion card, as part of a multifunction expansion card, or on a separate expansion card altogether, the following advertisements, along with their English translations, explains how you can add additional ports to your computer.

VESA IDE, SCSI-2, w/Multi-IO
This expansion card:
• Plugs into a VESA local bus expansion slot
• Supports an IDE hard drive
• Comes with an SCSI port
• Most likely includes a serial and a parallel port as well, although "Multi-IO" could mean anything the manufacturer wants it to

Dual-Port game card
This expansion card:
• Has two game ports

VESA SCSI-2 and LAN controller
This expansion card:
• Plugs into a VESA local bus expansion slot
• Has an SCSI port
• Has a network port

Multi-I/O card with serial & parallel ports
This expansion card:
• Has one or more serial ports
• Has one or more parallel ports

Super IDE 2HD/2FD 2S/1P/1G ports
This expansion card:
• Can control an IDE hard disk
• Can control up to two hard disk and two floppy disk drives
• Includes two serial ports, one parallel port, and one game port

4-Port serial card
This expansion card:
• Provides four serial ports

Before buying any expansion card, make sure you really need it. For example, some motherboards have built-in serial and parallel ports, and some video adapter cards may include a serial or parallel port. By combining your ports with items you already have (video adapter card, hard disk controller, etc.) you can avoid plugging up all your expansion slots.

To help you identify all the ports in your computer, use the following checklist:

Port Checklist

Serial ports:
    ❏ Mouse   ❏ External modem
    ❏ Printer   ❏ Network

How many:
_____

Parallel ports:
    ❏ Printer   ❏ External modem

How many:
_____

Game Ports:
    ❏ Joystick

How many:
_____

SCSI ports:
    ❏ External hard disk drive   ❏ External tape backup unit
    ❏ External CD-ROM drive

Network ports:
    ❏ Network

Warranty:
    ❏ 3 Year   ❏ 2 Year
    ❏ 1 Year   ❏ 30 Days

Dealer:
_____

Price:
_____

The typical computer needs two serial ports (one for a mouse and one for an external modem) and one parallel port (for a printer). The ideal solution is to find a motherboard that offers all of these ports built in. The second best solution is to buy a multifunction expansion card that offers one or more serial/parallel/game ports. The worst solution is to buy a separate expansion card for each type of port that you need.

9
Input devices

The two most common input devices are keyboards and mice, although scanners, trackballs, and speech recognition systems fall under this category as well. While most input devices consume almost no electricity, they can directly affect your wrists, hands, and arms.

Poorly designed keyboards are partly responsible for repetitive motion injuries like carpal tunnel syndrome. Because the most energy-efficient computer can still damage your hands if you use a poorly designed keyboard, you need to choose input devices that minimizes your risk and maximizes your comfort while you use your computer.

Choosing a keyboard

The most common input device is a keyboard. Because the keyboard is the one input device you'll use most often, the first thing to look for in a keyboard is its keys. The cheaper keyboards have the letters painted on top of the keys, while the better quality ones have the letters physically bonded as part of the key itself.

Brush your fingers lightly over the tops of any keyboard's keys. If you can feel the raised images of the letters under your fingertips, that means the letters have been painted on top of the keys. After prolonged use, these letters will gradually wear off, leaving the most commonly used keys smeared or completely blank.

The touch of the keys can be important as well. Some keyboards feel mushy, like touching a soggy dinner roll. Others have a firm, but annoying, clickety sound each time you press them. When comparing keyboards, press a few keys and test the feel. Two popular manufacturers of keyboards include Lexmark International (the makers of IBM keyboards) and Northgate OmniKey keyboards. In fact, Northgate even has a special technical support hotline just for answering questions about their keyboards.

Besides the touch and feel of individual keys, keyboards also differ in their placement of certain keys, like the function keys, Esc, Ctrl, Alt, and Caps Lock keys. The older AT-style keyboards put the function keys along the left side of the keyboard. The newer 101-style keyboards put the function keys on top of the keyboard.

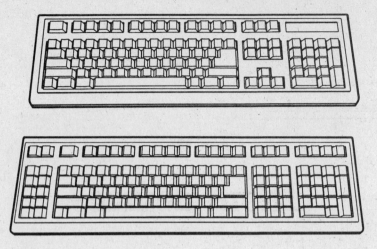

9-1 Common styles of keyboards.

Because some people prefer the function keys at the top of the keyboard while others prefer them along the left side, a few keyboards provide function keys along both the top and the left side. For those who really want a custom keyboard, some programmable keyboards let you remap keys. Instead of pressing two keys like Shift-F6, a custom keyboard would let you program a single key that represents this same keystroke combination.

The actual placement of the letter keys can affect your hands and wrists as well. The most common keyboard arrangement is one called QWERTY, which represents the first six letters in the top-left row of the keyboard. Although most people learn to type using the QWERTY layout, some people prefer the Dvorak layout.

Unlike the QWERTY layout, the Dvorak layout puts the most frequently used letters on the home row keys, minimizing the number of times you need to move your fingers to other parts of the keyboard. Proponents of the Dvorak layout claim that the average typist can type up to 20 percent faster using a Dvorak keyboard instead of a traditional QWERTY keyboard.

Unfortunately, Dvorak keyboards are rare. If you want one, you'll have to special order it. As an alternative, some programmable keyboards let you remap your entire keyboard to match the Dvorak layout, or you can buy special utility programs that will remap the keyboard for you. Of course, if you remap the keyboard, the letters on the keys will no longer match the letters that appear when you press each key.

Perhaps more damaging than constantly moving your fingers on a QWERTY layout is the physical placement of the user's hands and wrists on the keyboard. Most keyboards force the user's hands to work at an awkward angle, putting unnatural amounts of stress on the wrist.

To avoid these problems, you can buy special keyboard pads that lay in front of the keyboard, letting you rest your wrists comfortably in front. While such a keyboard pad adjusts the vertical motion of your wrists, it does nothing to help the horizontal motion of your wrists.

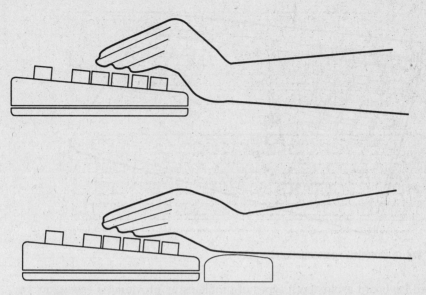

9-2 Side view of someone typing at a sharp angle of typing and a more natural angle.

9-3 Top view of someone typing at an unnatural angle and a more natural angle on an ergonomic keyboard.

Most keyboards align keys in neat parallel rows, as if everyone held their hands in front of them in a perfect straight line. Instead, most people hold their wrists at a slight angle to the keyboard. To accommodate this natural position of the wrists, a company called Marquardt Switches makes a keyboard that not only includes a built-in wrist-rest, but also angles the separate halves of the keyboard out.

In most keyboards, the thumbs do nothing more important than press the space bar. In Kinesis's ergonomic keyboard, the thumbs have separate keys of their own, increasing typing speed while also increasing user comfort.

Perhaps the most radical idea of all comes from a product called the BAT chord keyboard, from a company called InfoGrip. Because keyboard-related injuries occur when fingers move constantly and when wrists are placed in awkward angles, the

9-4 A Kinesis Ergonomic keyboard.

BAT chord keyboard avoids both types of problems by providing a seven-key keyboard with a built-in wrist-rest.

Four of the keys remain under the fingers at all times while the other three keys are controlled by the thumb. To type the most commonly used letters, you press one of the keys. To type less common letters, like Q, Z, or X, you press two or more keys simultaneously as a "chord." Because your fingers never move off the keys, the chance of repetitive stress injuries is effectively eliminated. Even better, a single BAT chord keyboard replaces an entire QWERTY keyboard, letting people continue using their computer with only one hand.

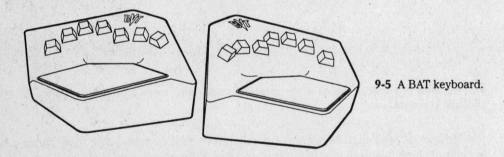

9-5 A BAT keyboard.

Of course, the more radical the keyboard design, the more time required to master it and the less likely people will be willing to try. With so many keyboard designs available, you have no excuse for not finding one that exactly meets whatever standards you might have.

Choosing a mouse

Like a keyboard, a mouse is a necessity to comfortably use most of today's programs. While it's possible to use OS/2 or Microsoft Windows strictly from the keyboard, it can get awkward and tiresome to press so many different keys just to perform a single command. That's why most computers these days need both a keyboard and a mouse.

Mice come in different physical types, depending on the connecting plug between the mouse and the computer:

- Serial mice
- Bus mice
- PS/2 mice
- Two- and three-button mice
- Ergonomic mice

A serial mouse gets its name because it plugs directly into a computer's serial port. If you don't have a spare serial port, you can't use a serial mouse. Because serial ports come in two different sizes (9 pin and 25 pin) and sexes (male and female), make sure your mouse can plug directly into your computer's serial port. Otherwise you may have to buy a special serial port adapter. As an alternative to a serial mouse, you may want to consider buying a bus mouse.

A bus mouse comes with its own expansion card that plugs into your computer's expansion slot. Then the bus mouse plugs directly into the back of the expansion card. Bus mice are more expensive than serial mice and use up a precious expansion slot in your computer. The main advantage is that a bus mouse frees up your computer's serial port for other uses.

For the advantage of a bus mouse without the drawback of using an expansion slot, some motherboards offer a built-in PS/2 mouse port. The drawback of this type of mouse is that most mice on the market are designed to plug into serial ports, so you may need to buy a special adapter to plug a serial mouse into a PS/2 port.

Both serial mice and bus mice work by measuring the movement of a ball, embedded inside the mouse. When you move the mouse, the ball inside rolls. Unfortunately, dirt can cause this ball to jam and slick surfaces can make the ball skip.

Once you've decided on the type of mouse to get (serial, bus, or PS/2), another consideration is the number of buttons that the mouse offers. Mice have two or three buttons, although most programs only use the left mouse button. As more people become comfortable using a mouse, many programs now include special uses for the right mouse button as well. Because most programs expect users to have a two-button mouse, the middle button of a three-button mouse often goes unused. Three-button mice, made by Logitech, lets you program "chords" so you can give multiple commands by pressing mouse button combinations. For maximum freedom of movement, a few mice eliminate the cord altogether and offer infrared or radio transmissions instead. Unfortunately, infrared mice require a clear line of sight to the computer. Even a single floppy disk in the way can cut the mouse off from the computer. Radio transmission mice don't require a clear line of sight to the computer, but they do suffer from the problem of interference with other radio-controlled mice, or even with any TV sets or stereos nearby.

The latest development in mice concerns ergonomics. The early mice were little more than an ugly box that felt as comfortable as moving a brick in your hand. The latest mice sport soft, rounded corners, curved bodies to support your palms, and finger indentations for maximum comfort. The newest ergonomic mice even come in models for left- or right-handed people.

Logitech has gone so far as to make a mouse specially designed for children. This kid's mouse is small enough for children's hands and looks like a real mouse. Even better, this kid's mouse lets you plug an ordinary mouse to it as well, so you don't have to unplug the kid's mouse to use your normal mouse and vice versa.

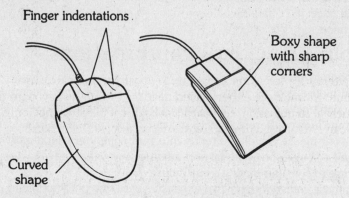

Finger indentations

Boxy shape with sharp corners

Curved shape

9-6 An ergonomic mouse compared to an ordinary mouse.

No matter what type of mouse you buy, make sure it's Microsoft Mouse compatible. If you buy a mouse that isn't Microsoft Mouse compatible, you may find that your mouse won't work with certain programs.

Although mice have become common enough that nearly every computer needs one, mice have the inherent disadvantage of requiring a fixed amount of space so you can move the mouse around. Many people also find a mouse cumbersome to use because you have to slide the mouse around to use it. Rather than bother with a mouse, some people choose to use a trackball instead.

Trackballs

Trackballs work like upside-down mice. Instead of the ball rolling along the flat surface of a desk, you spin the ball with your fingers or thumb and press buttons along the side of the trackball with your fingers.

Because trackballs don't require as much space as a mouse, they're often more convenient to use. For maximum comfort, Logitech sells the Trackman, where the

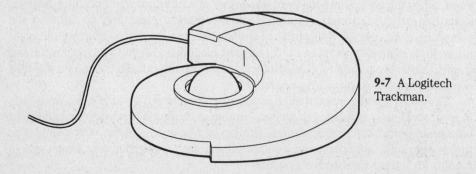

9-7 A Logitech Trackman.

trackball rests under the user's right thumb and the first three fingers of the right hand rest on three mouse buttons. (Too bad if you're left-handed, though.)

Like mice, trackballs usually plug into the serial port of your computer. For maximum comfort, the balls used in trackballs come in different sizes. Some people prefer small trackballs, while others prefer larger ones for greater control. Typical sizes of trackballs include 16 and 25 millimeters.

Keyboard/trackball combinations

As an alternative to buying a separate keyboard and trackball, many keyboards include a built-in trackball, either placed near the top of the keyboard or near the bottom. Such a combination keyboard/trackball combination not only saves you space, but can also prove more comfortable than a separate trackball.

Trackball

9-8 A combination keyboard/trackball.

With a separate trackball or mouse, you have to move one hand completely off the keyboard to use it. With a keyboard/trackball combination, you may just have to shift your hand a few inches to use the trackball. The less movement you have to do, the less possibility you'll strain your wrist and hand muscles.

Even more curious are unique keyboard/trackball alternative combinations. Rather than provide a built-in trackball, certain IBM keyboards include a special pointer device, called a TrackPoint II embedded between the G and H keys. The TrackPoint II looks and feels like a rubbery pencil eraser. Wherever you point it, that's the direction the mouse cursor moves.

The mouse buttons appear under the space bar, letting your thumbs conveniently reach and press them. By using a TrackPoint II keyboard, you can control your mouse cursor without moving your hand away from the home row keys of the keyboard.

Another odd alternative is a special pointer device embedded as the J key, which works like IBM's TrackPoint II device. When you press the J key normally, the letter J appears on the screen. But when you press the J key as a pointer device, it moves the mouse cursor around the screen.

Such alternative pointer devices/keyboards combinations can save space and let you work more conveniently than a separate mouse or trackball. Even better from a "green" point of view, these combination keyboard/pointer devices don't require any more additional packaging than an ordinary keyboard. KeyTronic even offers a

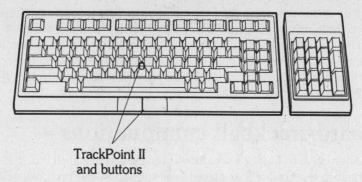

TrackPoint II
and buttons

9-9 The TrackPoint II embedded in a keyboard.

combination wrist rest and trackball that you place in front of your keyboard. The wrist rest keeps your hands at the proper angle for maximum comfort, while the trackball is conveniently located directly below both your thumbs. Using such a wrist rest/trackball combination minimizes hand movement, reducing the possibility of wrist injuries.

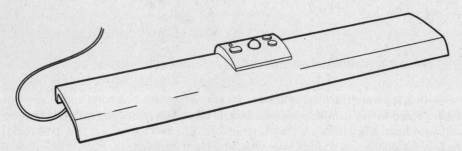

9-10 A combination wrist rest/trackball.

Alternate input devices

If you prefer, you can have a pointing device separate from the keyboard. Many companies sell touch-sensitive pads that lay flat on your desk. Instead of raising your hand and pointing at the screen, you just doodle on the touch-sensitive pad, which more closely mimics doodling on a sheet of paper.

For those who feel more comfortable using a pen instead of a computer, you can buy a pen-mouse. This device mimics the shape of a pen, but as you roll the tip along the surface, it moves the cursor across the screen. A button on the pen mimics a mouse button.

As a final alternative to using a mouse, you can now buy voice recognition systems that let you give verbal commands to your computer. (Of course, people have been giving verbal commands to their computers for years, but computers have never properly understood four-letter words.)

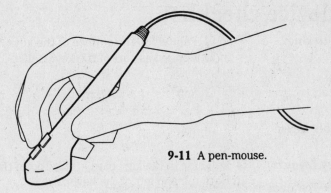

9-11 A pen-mouse.

Unfortunately, voice recognition systems are far from perfect, often getting confused between similar sounding words ("for" and "four"), getting confused from nearby noises, or failing to recognize your voice commands completely. Voice recognition may be the technology of the future, but for the present, it's too unreliable and expensive for everyday use.

Touch screens

Touch screens let you avoid a mouse or trackball altogether and use your finger to point instead. Initially, touch screens might look like the perfect solution because pointing is something that everyone can do naturally. For children, the disabled, or special uses like kiosks, touch screens can be the perfect solution. For everyday use, touch screens may not be as useful.

Touching a screen consistently requires raising your hand repeatedly and holding it at arm's length away from you. After several minutes of use, the finger you point at the touch screen may no longer be your index finger. Extended use of a touch screen tends to tire the arm and shoulder muscles.

Touch screens may also lack the precision that a mouse or trackball can give you. Pointing to a menu is easy enough with your finger, but try editing a length word processor document or calculating several spreadsheets. Unlike a mouse or trackball, a touch screen forces your hand to block your view of the screen, which can be inconvenient at best and completely annoying at worst.

For special uses like an information kiosk or as a computerized cash register, touch screens can be excellent replacements to mice or trackballs. But for normal use, consider the pros and cons of a touch screen before you buy one. Touch screens may be useful, but they won't replace mice and trackballs for most people's needs.

Shopping for a keyboard and a mouse

Every computer needs a keyboard and a mouse. To help you shop for a keyboard and pointing device (mouse, trackball, etc.), use the following checklist:

Input device checklist

Keyboard lettering:
- ❏ Painted on the surface of the keys
- ❏ Bonded as part of the key itself

Keyboard feel:
- ❏ Soft   ❏ Hard

Programmable keys:
- ❏ Yes   ❏ No

Function key layout:
- ❏ Left side of the keyboard   ❏ Top of the keyboard
- ❏ Both top and left of the keyboard

Keyboard layout:
- ❏ QWERTY layout   ❏ Dvorak layout
- ❏ Alternative layout

Built-in wrist-rest:
- ❏ Yes   ❏ No

Adjustable angle:
- ❏ Yes   ❏ No

Built-in pointing device:
- ❏ Trackball   ❏ TrackPoint II Mouse key None

Pointing device connection:
- ❏ Serial   ❏ Bus
- ❏ None

Pointing device type:
- ❏ Mechanical   ❏ Radio-controlled
- ❏ Infrared

Microsoft Mouse compatible: ❏ Yes   ❏ No

Warranty:
- ❏ 3 Year   ❏ 2 Year
- ❏ 1 Year   ❏ 30 Days

Dealer:
_____

Price:
_____

The following lists manufacturers that sell ergonomic keyboards, mice, track-balls, and pointing devices.

Keyboard manufacturers

ErgonomiXX, Inc.
525-K East Market Street
Box 295
Leesburg, VA 22075
Tel: (703) 771-1047
Fax: (707) 771-1137

Green Rating: *
(One star for ergonomic design)

Comments: The ErgonomiXX keyboard contains a built-in trackball, wrist rest, and keyboard split in half at an angle for maximum comfort. In addition, the function keys are arranged in a wheel shape instead of the traditional parallel rows of keys.

Health Care Keyboard Company
N82 W15340 Appleton Avenue
Menomonee Falls, WI 53051
Tel: (414) 253-6333
Fax: (414) 253-6330

Green Rating: *
(One star for ergonomic design)

Comments: The Health Care Keyboard is a normal keyboard divided into three parts. For maximum comfort, you can split the keyboard apart, and rotate and tilt the individual parts for your most comfortable hand and wrist posture.

IBM
Building 203
3039 Cornwallis Road
Research Triangle Park,
NC 27709
Tel: (800) 426-2968

Green Rating: **
(One star for ergonomic design)
(One star for donating to environmental causes)

Comments: The IBM TrackPoint II keyboard contains a tiny pointing device, embedded between the G and H keys, that looks like a tiny eraser head. The mouse buttons are at the bottom of the keyboard, within easy reach of either thumb. If you use an IBM ThinkPad laptop computer, you'll already be familiar with the TrackPoint II.

InfoGrip, Inc.
1145 Eugenia Place
Suite 201
Carpinteria, CA 93013
Tel: (805) 566-1049
Fax: (805) 566-1079

Green Rating: *
(One star for ergonomic design)

Comments: The BAT chord keyboard is one of the more unique keyboard designs in that it only requires one hand to use. You can buy one BAT chord keyboard for each hand if you want. Learning to use the BAT chord keyboard may take time, but it's the only keyboard that practically eliminates the risk of repetitive injuries because your hand and fingers remain in one place.

Jefferson Computer Products, Inc.
2901 N.E. 86th Street
Vancouver, WA 98665-0164
Tel: (206) 573-0624
Fax: (206) 573-0260

Green Rating: *
(One star for ergonomic design)

Comments: This company sells the Starpoint-101 keyboard, especially designed for touch typists. Basically it's an ordinary keyboard, but the letter keys double up as the cursor and numeric keypad. In this way, you can keep your fingers on the home row keys without moving your hands around. By minimizing excessive hand motion, the Starpoint-101 keyboard helps reduce the risk of repetitive stress injuries.

KeyTronic Corporation
P.O. Box 14687
Spokane, WA 99214-0687
Tel: (509) 928-8000
Fax: (509) 927-5383

Green Rating: *
(One star for ergonomic design)

Comments: KeyTronic was one of the first keyboard manufacturers to offer durable, high-quality replacement keyboards for IBM compatible computers. They sell a variety of different keyboards. Some include a built-in trackball while others are standard keyboards.

Lexmark International, Inc.
740 New Circle Road
Lexington, KY 40511-1876
Tel: (606) 232-2000

Green Rating: *
(One star for ergonomic design)

Comments: IBM used to own Lexmark, so it's not surprising that Lexmark sells the same keyboards as IBM. Unlike IBM, Lexmark also sells keyboards with built-in trackballs as well.

Marquardt Switches
2711 Route 20 East
Cazenovia, NY 13035
Tel: (315) 655-8050
Fax: (315) 655-8042

Green Rating: *
(One star for ergonomic design)

Comments: The Marquardt keyboard is fixed at a slight angle for ergonomic positioning of the hands and arms. For those who need a numeric keypad, Marquardt sells an optional numerical keypad that you can place on either the right or left side of the keyboard.

Northgate Computer Systems
7075 Flying Cloud Drive
Eden Prairie, MN 55344
Tel: (800) 453-0129

Green Rating: *
(One star for ergonomic design)

Comments: Northgate sells their OmniKey keyboards, which offer function keys on either the top or left side of the keyboard. One OmniKey model has function keys along both the top and left side of the keyboard with the ability to program specific keys.

Mouse/trackball manufacturers

Appoint
4473 Willow Road, #110
Pleasanton, CA 94566
Tel: (510) 463-3003
Fax: (510) 463-3204

Green Rating: *
(One star for ergonomic design)

Comments: Appoint makes a MousePen, which resembles an actual pen, and a tiny mouse called Gulliver, which you can flip over and use as a trackball.

Axelen
15621 S.E. 11th Street
Bellevue, WA 98008-5009
Tel: (206) 643-2781
Fax: (206) 643-4478

Green Rating: **
(One star for ergonomic design)
(One star for using recycled packaging)

Comments: Axelen sells a variety of mice and trackballs that have the unique ability to power down a monitor if you haven't touched the mouse after a certain period of time.

Kensington Microware
2855 Campus Drive
San Mateo, CA 94403
Tel: (415) 572-2700

Green Rating: *
(One star for ergonomic design)

Comments: The Kensington Expert Mouse is actually a huge trackball. As part of the package, Kensington provides a program that lets you customize the mouse cursor size, speed, and shape. In addition, the software also lets you reprogram the trackball buttons to represent multiple keystrokes. For example, you can define one button as the left mouse button and the second button to represent a double-click.

KeyTronic Corporation
P.O. Box 14687
Spokane, WA 99214-0687
Tel: (509) 928-8000
Fax: (509) 927-5383

Green Rating: *
(One star for ergonomic design)

Comments: KeyTronic sells a unique mouse (dubbed the Honeywell Mouse because it was originally developed by Honeywell) that uses two disks instead of a ball to measure movement. As a result, this mouse avoids the problems of slipping and dirt that can affect other types of mice. The company also sells a unique wrist pad that has a trackball embedded in the center. The wrist pad keeps your wrists straight for use on the keyboard while the trackball can be reached with either thumb, eliminating the need to move your hands off the keyboard.

Logitech, Inc.
6505 Kaiser Drive
Fremont, CA 94555
Tel: (510) 795-8500
Fax: (510) 792-8901

Green Rating: *
(One star for ergonomic design)

Comments: Logitech probably sells the widest variety of mice for any possible situation. They sell both right and left-handed mice, a mouse specially designed for kids, and a radio-operated cordless mouse. Nearly all Logitech mice have three buttons. Because the middle button is rarely used, Logitech supplies a program that lets the middle button emulate double-clicking the left mouse. Because beginners often have trouble double-clicking, this feature can make the Logitech mouse much easier to use.

Microsoft Corporation
One Microsoft Way
Redmond, WA 98052
Tel: (206) 882-8080
Fax: (206) 936-7329

Green Rating: **
(One star for ergonomic design)
(One star for in-house recycling programs)

Comments: Microsoft sells both a mouse and a trackball device designed especially for laptop computers. The latest Microsoft Mouse is slightly curved in the shape of a J, to conform to your hand. Unfortunately, this mouse is designed for right-handed users only. Left-handed users either have to adjust or use a different mouse altogether.

Mouse Systems Corporation
47505 Seabridge Drive
Fremont, CA 94538
Tel: (510) 656-1117
Fax: (510) 770-1924

Green Rating: *
(One star for ergonomic design)

Comments: Mouse Systems makes mice specially designed for CAD applications. The company also sells a range of lower-priced mice for normal business use.

Touch screen manufacturers

Keytec, Inc.
1293 N. Plano Road
Richardson, TX 75081
Tel: (214) 234-8617
Fax: (214) 234-8542

Green Rating: *
(One star for ergonomic design)

Comments: Keytec sells a variety of touch screens, including customized touch screens built to your requirements. Their touch screens simply attach to the front of any monitor and lets you run all mouse-driven programs with your finger or round-tipped stylus. Although the touch screen mimics a mouse or trackball, it won't support any program features that use the right mouse button.

10
Modems and fax boards

Modems and fax boards are completely optional. Most people can use a computer for years without ever needing a modem or fax board. But for more people, a modem and a fax board is slowly becoming a necessity. Best of all from a "green" point of view, modems and fax boards let you send information electronically to others, without wasting a single sheet of paper.

A modem lets your computer trade files with another computer located next door, across the city, on the other side of the country, or on the other side of the world. With a modem, you can exchange messages with any type of a computer, from an Apple Macintosh and a Commodore Amiga to an IBM mainframe or a Cray supercomputer. As long as two computers have a modem and a telephone line, they can communicate with one another.

Although modems are a luxury, they can make your computer much more useful by letting you trade programs with other people, get the latest stock market listings, or shop electronically. Some of the more common uses for a modem are for:

- Connecting to a local electronic bulletin board system (BBS)
- Connecting to an on-line service like CompuServe, Prodigy, or America On-Line
- Connecting two computers for transferring files

Electronic bulletin boards are simply personal computers that individuals or businesses set up for the enjoyment of anyone who calls. Bulletin boards usually have a theme, like programming, game playing, business development, or ecology. Because anyone can start a bulletin board with nothing more than a modem and a computer, almost every major city in America has close to one hundred bulletin boards to choose from. To find a list of bulletin boards near you, pick up a copy of *Computer Shopper* magazine or *BoardWatch* magazine, or ask members of a local computer user group for a list of BBS numbers.

Some bulletin boards are private and require a donation. Others let anyone call and copy files with no charge. No matter where you live, you'll likely find a bulletin board that will meet your needs.

For many people, on-line services like CompuServe, GEnie, or Prodigy are more useful because they offer a wide range of services from electronic shopping and stock trading to massive libraries of files to copy and special interest groups where you can swap ideas with people from around the world.

Such on-line services charge a fee to use, billed by the minute. Because some of these on-line services are so seductive to use, you can quickly rack up a huge bill if you're not careful.

Instead of dialing into other people's computers, many people need to dial into their own computer. For example, many consultants use special remote-control programs that let them dial into another computer and take control of it. Your computer could be in Jamaica and the consultant could be in Paris, but every key the consultant presses in Paris would appear like magic on your screen in Jamaica.

The purpose of such remote-control software is to let people modify, fix, or transfer files from one computer to another without physically being there. For example, rather than lug around huge amounts of files on a laptop computer all the time, a salesman could simply dial the office computer from a laptop computer and copy the necessary files he needs at the time.

If you need any of these capabilities, then you need a modem. When choosing a modem, look for the following features:

- Hayes compatibility
- Internal or external modems
- Modem speed
- Error control standards
- Data compression standards
- Fax capabilities
- Bundled software

Hayes compatibility

Almost every modem in the world follows a standard set of commands known as the Hayes command set. Sometimes modems will blatantly advertise the obvious and state "Hayes compatible" or sometimes they'll be more subtle and claim "Hayes AT command set."

In either case, make sure any modem you buy is Hayes-compatible. If you buy a modem that isn't Hayes-compatible (which is rare), then your modem won't be able to communicate with any other Hayes-compatible modems that people may be using.

Internal vs. external modems

Modems can be internal or external. From a "green" point of view, internal modems are better because they are less expensive, don't require a separate power supply, and don't require an external case. Internal modems just plug into your computer's ISA or EISA expansion slot. As far as your computer is concerned, the internal modem is just another serial port.

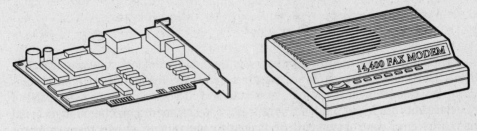

10-1 Comparison of an internal and an external modem.

External modems usually cost slightly more than internal modems, but can be used with more than one computer. If you have a Macintosh and an IBM-compatible computer, you could share an external modem between the two of them, something that would be impossible to do with an internal modem.

Modem speed

Modem speed is measured in baud or sometimes in bits per second (bps). Typical baud rates for modems are:

- 1200 baud
- 2400 baud
- 9600 baud
- 14,400 baud
- 19,200 baud
- 28,800 baud

The faster the baud rate, the less time you'll waste connected to the phone line. If you plan to use a modem on a regular basis, get the fastest modem possible. You'll more than save the extra cost of the modem in reduced telephone connect charges.

To connect to another computer, both computers must have a modem that works at the same baud rate. If you have a 9600-baud modem but your friend across the country only has a 2400-baud modem, then you'll both have to communicate at 2400 baud. As long as you have a fast modem, you can always slow down to match the speed of a slower modem.

Every few years, the standard for baud rates increases. Back in the mid-eighties, 1200 baud was standard. Near the end of the eighties, 2400 baud became standard. In the early nineties, 9600 baud became the standard and now 14,400 baud has become the new standard. While you can still pick up slower modems for bargain prices, your best bet is to buy a fast modem.

Error control standards

Modems that run at 9600 baud or higher may lose data over ordinary phone lines. To prevent data loss at high speeds, modems use special error control methods. The four types of error control standards are:

- MNP 4
- V.32
- V.32bis
- V.42

The MNP 4 error control standard was the first and oldest standard available. The V.32bis and V.42 standards are the latest standards. To use an error control standard, both modems must use the same standard. If your modem uses the MNP 4 standard but your friend's modem only uses the V.42 standard, neither modem could use either error control standard. To maintain compatibility with as many different modems as possible, most modems can use one or more error control standards.

Data compression standards

To make data transferring even faster, most 9600 baud or higher modems also include data compression. Data compression (which is separate from any data compression programs you may use, like PKZIP, LHarc, or ARJ) crunches files so they take up less space and can transfer over the phone lines faster. The three types of data compression standards are:

- MNP 5
- V.42bis
- V.FC

For maximum compatibility, most modems use both the MNP 5 and the V.42bis data compression standards. The new high speed 19,200 and 28,800-baud modems generally follow the new V.32 turbo or V.Fast Class (V.FC) standard. Unfortunately, neither standard has been wholly adopted by the industry, so a compromise standard, dubbed V.34, has been proposed to merge the V.32 turbo and V.FC standards together.

But no matter which standard wins out, users will all benefit. By using data compression, modems can essentially double or even triple the amount of data they can transfer at any given time, saving connect charges.

Fax capabilities

Many modems now offer combination modem/fax capabilities. Basically, you use the modem to communicate with other people who have a modem, and you use the fax to communicate with people who only have a fax machine. If someone has both a modem and a fax machine, it's more convenient to transfer data through the modem instead of the fax.

When someone sends you a word processor document by modem, you can edit that document on your computer. If someone sends you that same word processor document as a fax, then your computer treats it as a graphic file instead. Fax capabilities can be part of a fax/modem combination or as a separate fax board. When shopping for fax capabilities, look for the following features:

- Fax speed
- Send/Receive capabilities

- Class standard
- Fax group standard

Many fax/modem combinations work at different speeds. For example, the modem may have a maximum speed of 2400 baud, but the fax has a maximum speed of 9600 baud. Some of the latest fax/modems avoid this confusion by having identical maximum speeds for both the fax and the modem. Fax boards may also be limited to the following:

- Send only
- Receive only
- Send and Receive

A send-only fax only lets you send faxes but never receive them. A receive-only fax lets you receive faxes but never send them. A send and receive fax lets you do both. Although the cost of send-only or receive-only may be less, the savings probably won't be worth it unless you already have a separate fax machine anyway.

More important than fax speed is the class standard, Class 1 or Class 2. The class category defines how the fax board works. A Class 1 fax board relies mostly on software to do the work while a Class 2 fax board relies mostly on the hardware. For maximum compatibility, most fax boards follow both Class 1 and Class 2 standards.

The group standard defines the transmission times and resolution of faxes. Group I and Group II standards are considered obsolete, so only look for fax boards that meet the Group III standard.

Bundled software

By themselves, modems are useless without software to control them. Modems need a communications program, while fax boards need fax software. Most software that's included with a modem or fax board is fairly weak, but it will be enough to get by until you can buy a better communications or fax program.

As a bonus, some fax boards include an optical character recognition (OCR) program that can convert fax transmissions into plain text files that you can edit later on a word processor. Such OCR programs often advertise 90% accuracy in converting fax transmissions into text, but the reality is more like 10% accuracy and 90% manual (and tedious) editing.

Deciphering modem and fax board advertisements

To help you shop for a modem and fax board, the following sample advertisements have been translated into plain English.

2400-baud int. w/Software

This modem:

- Has a maximum speed of 2400 baud
- Is an internal modem
- Comes with communications software

9600/2400-baud ext. Fax/Modem
This modem:
- Is an external modem
- Has both fax and modem capabilities
- The fax has a maximum speed of 9600 baud
- The modem has a maximum speed of 2400 baud

14.4 Kbps Internal V.32bis modem
This modem:
- Has a maximum speed of 14,400 baud
- Is an internal modem
- Follows the V.32bis protocol standard

V.42 Send/Receive Fax/Modem
This modem:
- Has fax send and receive capabilities
- Follows the V.42 error correction standard

V.32 & V.42bis Compatible Fax/Modem Internal
This modem:
- Follows the V.32 error correction standard
- Follows the V.42bis data compression standard
- Has both fax and modem capabilities
- Is an internal modem

2400 Internal with 9600 send/4800 receive fax modem
This modem:
- Is an internal modem
- Has fax and modem capabilities
- The modem has a maximum speed of 2400 baud
- The fax has a maximum speed of 9600 baud when sending
- The fax has a maximum speed of 4800 when receiving

With so many features in a modem, it's important you get the features you need. To help you shop for a modem, use the following checklist:

Modem checklist

Modem type:	Internal	❏ External
Hayes compatible:	❏ Yes	❏ No
Modem speed:	❏ 28,800	❏ 19,200
	❏ 14,400	❏ 9600
	❏ 2400	

| Error control standards: | ❏ MNP 4 | ❏ V.32 |
| | ❏ V.32bis | ❏ V.42 |

| Data compression standards: | ❏ MNP 5 | ❏ V.42bis |
| | ❏ V.Fast | ❏ Class (V.FC) |

| Fax capabilities: | ❏ Send only | ❏ Receive only |
| | ❏ Send/Receive | ❏ None |

| Fax class: | ❏ Class 1 | ❏ Class 2 |

| Fax group: | ❏ Group I | ❏ Group II |
| | ❏ Group III | |

| Fax receive speed: | ❏ 19,200 | ❏ 14,400 |
| | ❏ 9600 | ❏ 4800 |

| Fax send speed: | ❏ 19,200 | ❏ 14,400 |
| | ❏ 9600 | ❏ 4800 |

| Software included: | ❏ Communications software | ❏ Fax software |
| | ❏ None | |

| Warranty: | ❏ 3 Year | ❏ 2 Year |
| | ❏ 1 Year | ❏ 30 Days |

Dealer:

_____

Price:

_____

Besides choosing the fastest and least expensive modem, you also want one that requires less electricity than competing modems. The following two companies sell "green" fax/modem chips that only require 3.3 volts. By contacting these manufacturers, you can find out which specific products use these "green" fax/modem chips in their products.

V.Fast Class Modem Chips
Rockwell International Corp.
4311 Jamboree Road
Newport Beach, CA 92658-8902
Tel: (714) 833-4600

Green Rating: *
(One star for energy-conserving features)

Comments: The Rockwell International modem chip consumes 250 milliwatts in active mode and 15 milliwatts in sleep mode when the computer isn't being used.

YTM414 Fax Modem Chip
Yamaha Corporation of America
Systems Technology Division
981 Ridder Park Drive
San Jose, CA 95131
Tel: (408) 437-3133

Green Rating: *
(One star for energy-conserving
features)

Comments: The Yamaha fax modem chip consumes 60 milliwatts in active mode and 0 milliwatts in sleep mode when the computer isn't being used.

11
Sound cards

Although most IBM-compatible computers come with a built-in speaker, the sound quality from this speaker is about as clear as listening to Beethoven's symphonies through an AM transistor radio. For better-quality sound, more people are turning to separate sound cards.

Not everyone needs sound in their computer. For many people, sound is only important for playing games, but as business presentation, multimedia, and even spreadsheet and word processor programs start adding the ability to include voice annotation, sound cards are slowly changing from a luxury to a necessity. In the future, you can expect sound cards to become as common as hard disk drives, especially as voice recognition and speech synthesis systems emerge. But for now, sound cards make sense mostly for the growing CD-ROM market and multimedia applications.

Internal and external sound cards

Most sound cards plug into an ISA or EISA bus expansion slot. Unfortunately, not only must you have a free expansion slot available, but you may also have to set jumpers and configure the proper IRQ and DMA settings for your sound card. (Not a difficult task, just a time-consuming and tedious one.)

Some of the newer sound cards provide an installation program that automates much of this process, but many sound cards do not. In those cases, be prepared to experiment with different IRQ and DMA settings until the sound card starts working right.

External sound cards usually plug in to the parallel port of your computer. If you have another device connected to the parallel port, like a printer, many external sound cards have something called a "pass-through" feature. This means you can plug the external sound card into a parallel port and then plug another device directly into the external sound card so you won't need to get a second parallel port. An external sound card without a "pass-through" feature will require a spare parallel port.

More internal sound cards are available than external ones, but if you need sound on a laptop computer or if you need to move a sound card conveniently between two or more different computers, then you'll have no choice but to choose an external sound card.

Internal sound cards can have an 8-bit or 16-bit bus interface. If you just want to play games, 8-bit sound cards are less expensive and produce acceptable sound quality. For business use or for more advanced games, a 16-bit sound card will provide higher quality sound because it transfers twice as much data (16 bits vs. 8 bits) at any given time.

For even higher quality sound and speed, look for a sound card with a digital signal processor (DSP), which is a separate processor specifically designed for working with sound. Any sound card with a DSP will run faster than a comparable sound card without a DSP because your computer's CPU can work in tandem with the DSP. Sound cards without a DSP force the CPU to do everything, slowing down your computer and reducing sound quality considerably.

Sampling and playback

The true quality of any sound card depends on its sampling and playback capabilities. Sampling refers to the sound card's ability to translate sound waves into corresponding changes in electrical voltage levels. To digitize electrical signals, the sound board takes a series of rapid voltage measurements called samples. Two factors that affect the sound quality of any sound card are the sampling size and the sampling rate.

The sampling size defines the dynamic range of the recorded sound. The smaller the sampling size, the lower the quality recorded. Sampling sizes are measured in bits, ranging from a low of 8 bits to 10 bits, 12 bits, and 16 bits. Likewise, the sampling rate determines how frequently the sound is recorded. The higher the sampling rate, the higher the quality of sound. Sampling rates are measured in kilohertz (kHz); typical values are 11 kHz, 22 kHz, 44 kHz, and 48 kHz.

MIDI support

Most sound cards support the Microsoft standard .WAV sound files, which actually stores recorded sound on disk. Unfortunately, recording even a few minutes of sound can gobble up almost a megabyte of space. As an alternative, many sound cards also support MIDI files.

Unlike .WAV files, MIDI files contain don't contain the actual sound but digital instructions for recreating that sound. This is like the difference between a bakery full of pies and a cookbook with recipes that show you how to make any kind of pie. As a result, MIDI files are always much smaller than .WAV files.

Most (but not all) sound cards come with a MIDI synthesizer chip, but not all MIDI sound cards support the general MIDI standard. Those that do can playback MIDI files recorded by other sound cards. Those that don't can only play MIDI files recorded by others using the same sound card.

The sound quality of MIDI files is determined by the number of notes or voices the sound card can play simultaneously. The fewer the number of voices, the poorer the sound quality will be. Typical numbers of voices range from 11 up to 32.

If you want to create your own MIDI files using an external MIDI synthesizer, you'll need a sound card with a MIDI port. Some sound cards provide this as a standard feature, others provide it as an extra option, and some don't provide a MIDI port at all.

Recording capabilities

Besides playing back sound, sound cards also let you record and store new sounds. To record sounds, a sound card needs a microphone and an optional stereo line-in. To play back sound stored in a variety of .WAV files, MIDI files, or audio CD tracks, you also need a mixer. A mixer with two channels can only handle two separate sound sources, so the greater the number of mixer channels, the more flexible your recording capabilities will be.

As more sounds are stored on CD-ROM, more sound cards now provide CD-ROM support. With a CD-ROM interface, you can mix sounds directly off an audio CD-ROM, or even convert your $2,000 computer into a stereo system, letting you play music while you work.

Compatibility

Although the computer industry tries to enforce standards so equipment from different manufacturers can work together, the sound card industry is so new that multiple standards abound. Until a single standard dominates, it's best to get a sound card that follows two or more standards for maximum compatibility. Some of the most popular standards are:

- SoundBlaster
- Ad Lib
- MPC-2
- Disney Sound Source

For game-playing, the sound standard revolves around the SoundBlaster and Ad Lib sound cards. If you're planning to use games and educational programs from Walt Disney, these programs follow an entirely different standard called Disney Sound Source. For business applications, most programs follow the Multimedia PC specification (MPC).

Before buying a sound card, make sure your programs adhere to one of these standards. Otherwise you may get stuck with a sound card that doesn't work with any of your software.

Bundled software

Sound cards usually come with software to help you get started. Some common types of bundled software are:

- Installation programs
- Voice recognition
- Sound recording, editing and mixing
- Sound files

Installation programs help you set up your sound card for the first time. Many of these programs automatically configure the sound card to your computer by installing software drivers and setting IRQ and DMA addresses. (If you don't know what these are, that explains why installation programs are so popular.)

Voice recognition programs let you give verbal commands to your computer, and the sound card translates those commands into keystroke commands. While such voice recognition programs are far from accurate, they can be useful for the disabled or for simple commands like "Save" or "Exit." (Then again, imagine an office full of people telling their computers at the end of the day, "Quit," "Stop," or "Heel.")

Obviously, recording, editing, and mixing sound is impossible without appropriate software, so most sound cards include a program that does one or more of these functions. Because recording sound can be so troublesome on your own (how can you capture the sound of a 747 landing at an airport unless you drag your computer to the runway?), many sound cards include prerecorded sound files that you can use, edit, and mix with your own sounds.

Headphones and speakers

Of course, the quality of your sound card is ultimately determined by the quality of your speakers and headphones. Some sound cards include speakers and headphones, but most don't. And some sound cards only provide one jack, so you can either use headphones or speakers, not both at the same time. With only one jack, you'll have to constantly unplug the speakers and plug in the headphones, and vice versa, whenever you want to switch.

You can't use ordinary stereo speakers with your computer for two reasons. One, sound cards don't provide enough power for a home stereo speaker, so you need a speaker with a built-in amplifier. Two, speakers emit magnetic fields that can interfere with your monitor, so you need a shielded speaker. Some companies now sell speakers built-in to the computer case or the monitor. Generally the combination computer case/speaker or monitor/speaker is less expensive than buying the parts separately but less flexible because you can't position the speakers where they sound best.

Deciphering advertisements for sound cards

As the sound card market is still in its infancy, choosing a sound card can be more confusing than choosing a monitor or hard disk. The following shows typical sound card advertisements along with their English translations:

SCSI and MIDI Port, 32 stereo voices, 16 MIDI channels, 16-bit 44 kHz
This sound card:
- Includes an SCSI and MIDI port
- Has a MIDI chip with 32 voices
- Can mix up to 16 channels
- Uses a 16-bit sampling size
- Uses a 44-kHz sampling rate

16-bit/44-kHz Record/Playback, Yamaha OPL-3 stereo synthesis 20-voice chip, 100% Sound Blaster and Ad Lib compatibility
This sound card:
- Uses 16-bit sampling sizes
- Has a 44-kHz sampling rate
- Uses a Yamaha OPL-3 MIDI chip with 20 voices
- Runs all programs that require a Sound Blaster or Ad Lib sound card
To help you shop for a sound card, use the following checklist:

Sound card checklist

Sound card connection:
- ❏ Internal___-bit bus interface (8-bit or 16-bit)
- ❏ External parallel port connection

Sampling size:
- ❏ 16-bit   ❏ 12-bit
- ❏ 10-bit   ❏ 8-bit

Sampling rate:
- ❏ 44 kHz   ❏ 22 kHz
- ❏ 11 kHz

MIDI support:
- ❏ Yes   ❏ No

MIDI interface:
- ❏ Yes   ❏ No
- ❏ Optional

Number of MIDI voices:
- ❏ 32   ❏ 24
- ❏ 20   ❏ 18
- ❏ 11   ❏ 9
- ❏ None

Number of channels available for mixing:

_____

CD-ROM interface:
- ❏ Yes   ❏ No

Compatibility: ❑ SoundBlaster ❑ Ad Lib
❑ MPC ❑ Disney Sound Source

Bundled software: ❑ Installation ❑ Voice recognition
❑ Sound recording ❑ Sound editing
❑ Sound mixing ❑ Sound files

Headphones included: ❑ Yes ❑ No

Speakers shielded: ❑ Yes ❑ No

Warranty: ❑ 3 Year ❑ 2 Year
❑ 1 Year ❑ 30 Days

Dealer:

_____

Price:

_____

12
CD-ROM drives

As programs get bigger and include sound, video, and graphic files, more software will be distributed on CD-ROM. Just as hard disks changed from a luxury to a necessity, so CD-ROM drives will soon become necessary not only for game playing and multimedia applications, but for standard programs like word processors and databases.

Even companies like Microsoft, IBM, and Novell offer CD-ROM versions of certain programs. If your computer can't use CD-ROM, you immediately limit the capabilities of your computer. Some of the more common uses for CD-ROM disks are for:

- Distributing programs too bulky to fit on multiple floppy disks
- Storing massive amounts of shareware or demonstration programs to evaluate
- Storing large amounts of graphic, video, and sound clips
- Running multimedia applications like combination video/text encyclopedias

In the old days, entire word processors used to fit on a single 360K floppy disk. Nowadays, most programs require several 1.44MB floppy disks along with two or more hundred-page manuals. Since few people bother or need to read the entire manuals, many companies are distributing special versions of their programs on CD-ROM disks. Not only does this make installation more convenient, but the CD-ROM disk also contains on-line reference manuals, eliminating the need to print manuals.

Because of the sheer number of programs available, many companies sell CD-ROM disks containing several thousand shareware and commercial programs. At your leisure, you can copy any of these programs off the CD-ROM disk and evaluate it. If you like the program, you can send money to the publisher and they'll send you the printed manuals, or provide you with a code to unlock the manuals already stored on the CD-ROM disk.

Since multimedia applications are becoming more popular, the Multimedia Marketing Council, a consortium of various computer companies, has defined a multimedia standard called MPC Level 2. An MPC Level 2 computer must:

- Be an 80486SX running at 25MHz
- Have at least 4MB of RAM
- Have a hard disk of at least 160MB

- Have a 16-bit sound card with a 44-kHz sampling rate, a mixer capable of blending CD audio, digital audio, a synthesizer, and an auxiliary line
- Have a minimum of 640 × 480 screen resolution
- Have a CD-ROM drive with a 300Kbps transfer rate and an access speed of less than 400 ms

To help you choose a CD-ROM drive that meets the MPC Level 2 specification, here are some factors to consider.

Internal and external CD-ROM drives

CD-ROM drives can be internal or external. Internal drives require a drive bay, plus a controller card plugged into an expansion slot. Most external drives require a SCSI controller card, but a few plug directly into a parallel port. An external·drive also requires a separate power outlet which, from a "green" point of view, wastes additional electricity.

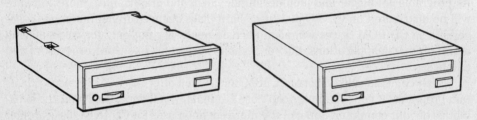

12-1 Differences between an internal and an external CD-ROM drive.

Access speed

Access speed determines how fast the CD-ROM can find specific information stored on the CD-ROM disk. The access speed is measured in milliseconds (ms), and typically ranges from 200 ms up to 400 ms. The higher the access speed, the slower your CD-ROM drive can find information.

Transfer rate

An even more important measure of a CD-ROM drive's speed is its transfer rate. The transfer rate determines how fast the CD-ROM can move information stored on the CD-ROM disk to the computer.

Transfer rates are measured in kilobytes per second (abbreviated as Kbps, K/sec, or just K). The slowest transfer rate you should consider is 150 Kbps. The newer CD-ROM drives have a 300 Kbps transfer rate, which makes CD-ROM programs run faster. Most CD-ROM drives with a 300 Kbps transfer rate can, if necessary, slow down to 150 Kbps. Such CD-ROM drives are called multispeed drives.

To boost transfer rate speeds even more, many CD-ROM drives come with a built-in cache, which typically ranges in size from 64K up to 256K. Given two CD-ROM drives with equivalent transfer rates, the one with the larger cache will be the faster of the two.

CD-ROM disk compatibility

Although CD-ROM technology has been around for years, the standards for storing data on a CD-ROM disk keep changing as new programs and computers appear on the market. Some of the more common CD-ROM disk standards are:

- ISO-9660
- CD-I
- CD-ROM XA
- Kodak Photo CD

The ISO-9660 standard has been around the longest. It was adapted from an even earlier standard called the High Sierra Format, which dates back to 1985. Because this is one of the oldest CD-ROM disk standards, nearly every CD-ROM drive and CD-ROM disk conforms to this specification.

The CD-I standard (which stands for CD-Interactive) was developed by Philips for their line of interactive consumer products, like television sets. This standard permits the mixing of sound, video, and text.

The CD-ROM XA standard (XA stands for eXtended Architecture) also permits the mixing of sound, video, and text, but also includes the ability to use an audio data compression standard called Adaptive Differential Pulse Code Modulation (AD-PCM). This data compression standard essentially quadruples the audio capacity of a CD-ROM disk.

The Kodak Photo CD standard was developed by (surprise!) Kodak and refers to special CD-ROM disks that let you store your own photographs on them. The idea is to let you take pictures with your own camera, take the film to a Kodak processing center, and they'll cheerfully store your photographs on the Kodak Photo CD for a nominal fee.

Each time you record photos to a Kodak Photo CD-ROM disk, it's called a session. Any CD-ROM disk that has been written to more than once is called a multisession CD-ROM disk. Older CD-ROM drives are only single session, but the newer ones are multisession CD-ROM drives.

Although many standards exist for CD-ROM disks, most commercially available CD-ROM disks follow the old ISO-9660 for maximum compatibility. If you plan to use Kodak Photo CD-ROM disks, then look for CD-ROM drives that also advertise "PhotoCD" or "multisession" compatibility.

Extra features to consider

Believe it or not, you can take ordinary music CD-ROM disks and play them in computer CD-ROM drives. Of course, to do that, your CD-ROM drive needs an audio jack and a volume control knob.

Some CD-ROM drives also require a special "caddy" that holds the CD-ROM disk, while other CD-ROM drives let you place the CD-ROM disk directly into the drive. A caddy protects your CD-ROM disks, but also requires the additional use of plastic to make them. From a "green" point of view, look for a CD-ROM drive that can use CD-ROM disks without a caddy.

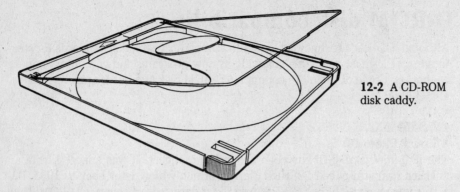

12-2 A CD-ROM disk caddy.

The procedure for inserting and removing a CD-ROM disk differs among CD-ROM drives. Some CD-ROM drives are motorized, which means that you press a button and (hopefully) the CD-ROM drive gobbles up or ejects the CD-ROM disk automatically. If the motor fails, the CD-ROM drive will have a special hole for (here's the high-tech solution) ramming a paper clip in to physically eject the CD-ROM disk.

Other CD-ROM drives are manually operated, requiring you to push and pull CD-ROM disks out yourself. Although neither motor or manual ejection mechanisms won't affect the performance of your CD-ROM drive, choosing one or the other depends on your own personal preferences.

Bundled programs

CD-ROM drives by themselves are worthless without a CD-ROM disk to use. As a special bonus, many CD-ROM drives come with bundled CD-ROM disks that you can use once you've installed your CD-ROM drive.

Such bundled CD-ROM disks usually include an encyclopedia, games, desktop publishing clip art, sound and video clip art, or marginally useful reference works like the CIA World Factbook or a history of the American Civil War.

Deciphering advertisements for CD-ROM drives

Because CD-ROM drives are relatively new, choosing the right CD-ROM drive can be confusing. Here are some sample CD-ROM drive advertisements along with their English translations:

CD-ROM XA Ready, Internal CD-ROM Drive, Photo-CD compat., Daisy chain
This CD-ROM drive is:
- Compatible with both the CD-ROM XA and Kodak Photo CD disk standards
- An internal CD-ROM drive
- Uses an SCSI controller card that lets you daisy chain multiple SCSI devices

Triple Speed, 450 KB/sec Transfer Rate, 256K Cache Buffer, SCSI
This CD-ROM drive:
- Can change its transfer rate speed from a maximum of 450 Kbps to 300 Kbps and 150 Kbps
- Includes a 256K cache
- Uses an SCSI controller card

Internal 280 ms w/Kodak Multisession
This CD-ROM:
- Is an internal CD-ROM drive
- Has an access speed of 280 ms
- Is compatible with the Kodak Photo CD standard

Double speed (307KB Transfer), Caddy free, includes 16-bit interface
This CD-ROM drive:
- Can change its transfer rate from a maximum of 307KB to 150KB
- Doesn't require the use of a caddy to use CD-ROM disks
- Includes a controller card as part of the purchase price

To help you shop for a CD-ROM drive, use the following checklist:

CD-ROM drive checklist

CD-ROM type: ❑ Internal ❑ External

Interface: ❑ SCSI ❑ Parallel Port

Access speed: _____ milliseconds (ms)

Transfer rate: ❑ 450 K / sec ❑ 300 K / sec
❑ 150 K / sec

Built-in cache: ❑ 256K ❑ 128K
❑ 64K ❑ None

CD-ROM disk compatibility: ❑ Kodak Photo CD ❑ CD-I
❑ CD-ROM XA ❑ ISO-9660

Caddy Required: ❑ Yes ❑ No

Headphone/speaker jacks: ❑ Yes ❑ No

Bundled CD-ROM disks:

_____

Warranty: ❏ 3 Year   ❏ 2 Year
                  ❏ 1 Year   ❏ 30 Days

Dealer:

_____

Price:

____

13
Printers

Every computer needs a printer, although the type of printer you get depends on what you need. The three most popular types of printers are:

- Laser printers
- Inkjet printers
- Dot-matrix printers

The "greenest" printers are dot-matrix printers, because they require very little electricity to run and require no supplies more complicated than an ink ribbon, which can be reused. Inkjet printers are the next "greenest" printers, because they require little electricity to run and have ink cartridges that can be reused and refilled. The least "green" printers are laser printers. Not only do they consume large amounts of electricity, even when idle, but they require large amounts of consumables (plastic cartridges, toner, printing drum, etc.).

However, laser printers excel at producing high-quality printing for standard size paper, forms, and envelopes. Inkjet printers mimic laser printers in printing capability and quality, but cost much less. For that reason, inkjet printers are becoming the most popular types of printers for personal use. Dot-matrix printers are the least expensive printers to buy and are the only types of printers that can print on wide paper or carbon paper to create multiple copies.

Printer emulation

No matter what type of printer you get, the most important feature is printer emulation. To make your computer work with your printer, your software must know how to use your printer. If you buy an oddball printer, your programs probably won't know how to use it.

Printer emulation means that your printer can fool your computer into thinking it's a more popular type of printer. Some of the more popular types of printers to emulate include Epson (for dot-matrix printers) and Hewlett-Packard (for inkjet and laser printers). The more printer emulations a printer offers, the more compatible it will be for a wide variety of computers.

Laser printers

Laser printers are becoming the new standard for computer printers. As prices hover around the $600 mark and print quality keeps increasing, more people are making a laser printer their first choice.

But not all laser printers are alike. Some features to look for in a laser printer include:

- The footprint
- Maximum printing resolution
- Printing speed
- Interface
- Number of built-in fonts and the ability to accept additional font cartridges
- Maximum amount of RAM
- PostScript support
- Power consumption when idle

Footprint

The footprint of a laser printer is, basically, the amount of desk area that it covers. The older model laser printers are relatively squat and wide. To conserve precious desktop space, the latest laser printers are tall and narrow, increasing the likelihood that you can tuck them away in an unused area of your desk (and also increasing the likelihood that you'll tip them over by mistake).

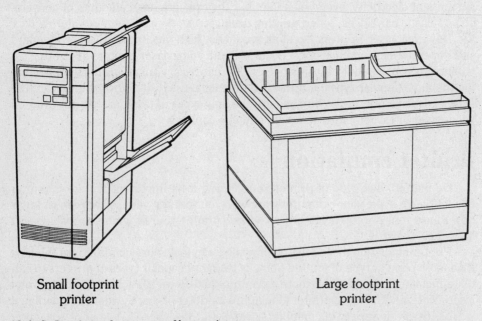

Small footprint
printer

Large footprint
printer

13-1 Comparison of two types of laser printers.

Print resolution and speed

The main feature of any printer is the quality of its printing. Laser printer resolution is measured in dots per inch (dpi), with common resolutions of 300, 400, 600, and 1200 dpi. The higher the dots per inch, the sharper the printing resolution.

Besides printing resolution, speed can also be a decisive factor in choosing one laser printer over another one. Speed is measured in pages per minute (ppm), and often is as wildly exaggerated as the miles per gallon claims found on automobiles. (Does anyone really get 40 miles to the gallon in city driving?) Typical printing speeds range from a low of 4 ppm to a high of 20 ppm.

Because printing speeds are usually estimated on the optimistic side, the actual printing speed will depend on the type of information you're printing out. For example, printing five pages of text will be much faster than printing five pages of graphic images.

Printer interfaces

For maximum compatibility, many laser printers offer a variety of interfaces for connecting the laser printer to your computer. Most laser printers offer a parallel and a serial port, and a few include an Apple LocalTalk port (for connecting the laser printer to a Macintosh) and an Ethernet port (for connecting the laser printer to a network). Laser printers with multiple printer interfaces often include interface switching, which lets the printer automatically switch between two or more computers.

For example, if you had a Macintosh and an IBM connected to the same printer, you wouldn't have to press any buttons or switches on the laser printer to switch it between the two computers. The moment someone started printing from the Macintosh, the laser printer would detect the printing and switch to the Apple LocalTalk port. The moment someone started printing from the IBM, the laser printer would switch to the parallel or serial port. If you're planning to connect and use several computers on the same laser printer at once, an automatic interface switching feature is definitely a feature to look for.

Fonts

To provide variety in printing, laser printers come with a fixed number of built-in fonts. If you want to print out a font that your laser printer doesn't provide, you have two choices. One, many laser printers accept special font cartridges that plug into the laser printer and provide additional fonts. Two, you can copy the necessary fonts from your computer and store them in your laser printer's own RAM.

Some laser printers only accept font cartridges specially designed for that particular laser printer. Other laser printers accept font cartridges designed for Hewlett-Packard laser printers. Because Hewlett-Packard-compatible font cartridges are more numerous and less expensive, look for a laser printer that can accept these font cartridges.

As an alternative to font cartridges, many laser printers include their own RAM, ranging from a low of 512K to a high of 32MB. The more RAM available, the more fonts you can store. If your laser printer doesn't come with enough RAM to suit your needs, you can expand your laser printer's RAM by adding standard SIMMs. Some laser printers can use ordinary SIMMs while others require different memory chips.

If you need desktop publishing capabilities, look for a laser printer with Post-Script support. Some laser printers come with PostScript built-in while others offer it only as an option. PostScript is a universal page description language used for printing fancy designs. If your printing needs are fairly simple, then you can safely avoid any PostScript options and save yourself some money.

"Green" laser printers

Laser printers are notorious for gobbling up electricity. Although Energy Star laser printers still consume over 150 watts of electricity while printing, they'll use less than 30 watts of power while idle. Besides reduced power usage, a few laser printers go even further towards conservation.

Most laser printers have a printer drum and toner cartridges that eventually wear out and need replacing. Because most of these discarded printer drums and toner cartridges wind up being dumped in landfills, the Kyocera Ecosys printer is notable for using a drum that lasts the lifetime of the printer and eliminating toner cartridges altogether. Instead of adding an entire toner cartridge, you just add toner. As an option for more traditional laser printers, you can use recycled toner cartridges.

A few laser printers even have a fax modem as an option. Instead of buying a separate fax machine that prints on waxy fax paper, these laser printer/fax combinations let you use ordinary paper for receiving faxes.

Finally, any laser printer can conserve resources a little bit more by using recycled paper. Recycled paper is rated according to its percentage of recycled fibers, ranging from a high of 100% to a low of 35%. See Appendix A for sources of recycled laser printer paper.

Inkjet printers

As a less expensive alternative to laser printers, many people buy an inkjet printer. An inkjet printer has several of the same advantages that make laser printers so attractive. Inkjet printers are quiet, print at resolutions rivaling laser printers, and some can print in color.

The main drawbacks of inkjet printers are that the ink sometimes smears on the paper, print quality is noticeably lower than comparable laser printers, and the ink cartridges cost more per page to print than laser printers. (The average cost per page of text is less than 1 cent per page for dot-matrix printers, 3 cents per page for laser printers, and 6 cents per page for inkjet printers.)

Differences between inkjet and laser printers

Although inkjet printers mimic laser printer features, there are a few noticeable differences. First of all, the print resolution of inkjet printers ranges from 300 dpi to 360 dpi, much lower than the 400 dpi or 600 dpi print resolutions of the latest laser printers.

Second, inkjet printers usually offer parallel or serial interfaces, but no AppleTalk or network support. This means that only one computer can be connected to an inkjet printer at a time, and you can't share an inkjet between an IBM and a Macintosh.

A third major difference lies with fonts. Many inkjet printers include built-in fonts and let you plug in additional font cartridges. Unfortunately, the font selection is usually less comprehensive than those found in laser printers, and inkjet printers generally lack enough memory to store fonts in RAM.

Rather than use built-in RAM for fonts, most inkjets use built-in RAM as a print buffer. Whenever you tell your computer to print something, your computer obediently sends all the data to the printer. Unfortunately, the computer can send data faster than the printer can print it out, which means that your computer spends most of its time waiting for the printer to finish.

An inkjet with a print buffer can store part of its data in its memory, freeing up the computer from waiting for the printer to finish. The larger the print buffer, the quicker it can free up the computer.

Along with the limited selection of fonts, inkjet printers also lack PostScript support. For people just writing reports and printing graphs, the absence of PostScript and extensive fonts won't matter. But for people who do desktop publishing, an inkjet printer simply can't replace a laser printer.

Probably the biggest advantage of an inkjet printer is its ability to print in color. Color laser printers are still way too expensive, and color dot-matrix printers produce fuzzy and blurry results. For that reason alone, inkjet printers will continue to dominate the color printer market until inexpensive color laser printers become available.

Dot-matrix printers

A dot-matrix printer is not only one of the least expensive types of printers you can buy, but also one of the most reliable. Basically, a dot-matrix printer is nothing more than a glorified typewriter that can grab and spit out fanfold paper. Because of their durability and low operating costs, dot-matrix printers are often used for high-volume work like printing forms, mailing labels, or rough drafts.

When shopping for a dot-matrix printer, you may see dot-matrix printers advertising the following features:
- Pin-type and print resolution
- Carriage width
- Paper feed mechanism
- Fonts
- Noise level rating

Pin-type and print resolution

A dot-matrix printer creates letters and graphics by using a multitude of tiny dots. Naturally, the more dots used, the higher the print quality. The pin-type refers to the number of pins that the dot-matrix printer uses.

The lowest number of pins used are 9-pin dot-matrix printers. The highest number of pins used are 24-pin dot-matrix printers. Although a 24-pin dot-matrix printer has a slightly higher print quality than a 9-pin dot-matrix printer, the difference may be negligible.

Dot-matrix printers usually offer two types of print quality: draft and near letter quality (NLQ). Draft quality is faster but produces less defined print. Near letter quality prints slower and produces printing that almost looks as if it came from a poorly built typewriter.

Carriage width

The carriage width refers to the maximum paper size the printer can use. While most inkjet and laser printers are limited to paper widths of 8.5 inches, wide-carriage dot-matrix printers can handle paper up to 17 inches wide.

The wider the carriage width, the more types of paper the printer can use. If you need to use different-sized paper, then a dot-matrix printer may be your only option. But if you will never print on paper wider than the standard 8.5 inches, then a wide-carriage printer will cost more without offering you any useful advantages.

Paper feed mechanism

The paper feed mechanism refers to the way the printer grips sheets of paper. Dot-matrix printers can typically use ordinary sheets of paper or special fanfold paper with holes along the edges to align the paper within the printer.

For ordinary sheets of paper, the dot-matrix printer simply uses the pressure of its rollers to guide the paper through the printer. For fanfold paper, dot-matrix printers use tractor feeds, which look like little sprockets that fit through the holes of fanfold paper and guide each page through the printer.

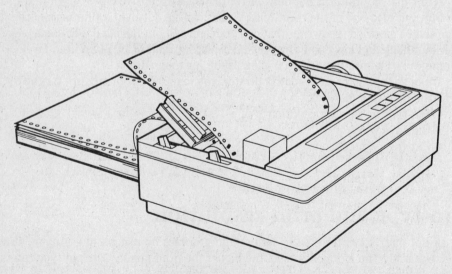

13-2 A tractor feeds works with fanfold paper.

Tractor feed mechanisms come in two varieties: push or pull. A push tractor feed shoves the paper into the printer from behind. A pull tractor feed pulls the paper into the printer from the front.

A printer with a pull tractor feed always starts printing on the second available page, because the pull tractor feed needs the first sheet of paper to pull the rest of the pages through the printer. A printer with a push tractor feed always starts printing on the first available page.

Unfortunately, push tractor feeds are more prone to jamming, because the paper may get bent feeding into the printer. Pull tractor feeds waste a sheet of paper each time you print, but they are usually less prone to jamming than push tractor feeds.

Fonts

Like inkjet printers, dot-matrix printers have a certain number of built-in or resident fonts. If you need more than the ones provided, you usually won't be able to add any through additional font cartridges or into the printer's RAM. If your work requires fonts, you should consider an inkjet or laser printer instead.

Noise levels

Unlike inkjet or laser printers, dot-matrix printers are noisy because they physically strike the page to print on it. As a result, dot-matrix printers tend to sound like little buzzsaws whenever they're printing. Some people isolate their dot-matrix printers in a separate room or cabinet to reduce the noise, but if you don't have this luxury, then you'll have to look at the noise level ratings of different printers.

Typical noise levels of dot-matrix printers range from a low of 40 decibels (dB) to a high of 60 decibels. To further reduce the annoyance of printing, many dot-matrix printers offer a standard printing mode and a special quiet printing mode. During the quiet printing mode, the printer prints slower and at a lower print quality.

Deciphering printer advertisements

Like most types of computer advertising, printer advertisements tend to assume that you already understand the technical jargon sprinkled liberally throughout. To help you understand printer advertisements, the following are common printer features found in advertisements:

KX-P4410 Laser Printer, 5 PPM print speed, 300 dpi, 200-sheet paper cassette tray, 512K RAM expands to 4.5MB, Parallel interface, 28 resident fonts, Power-save feature

This laser printer has the following features:
- A maximum printing rate of five pages per minute.
- A maximum print resolution is 300 dots per inch.
- A maximum paper capacity of 200 sheets of paper.
- A minimum of 512K of memory for storing fonts, but expandable all the way up to 4.5MB.

- The ability to connect to your computer's parallel port.
- 28 built-in fonts.
- The ability to reduce power consumption when not in use.

IBM Thermal Jet 4070, 110 cps draft/83 cps LQ, 360 dpi, 37K print buffer, eight resident fonts
This inkjet printer has the following features:
- A maximum printing speed of 110 characters per second in draft mode and 83 characters per second in letter quality (LQ) mode.
- A maximum print resolution of 360 dots per inch.
- 37K of built-in RAM to use as a print buffer.
- Eight built-in fonts.

GSX-190, 9-pin printer, 270 cps draft/40 cps LQ, eight resident fonts, 8K print buffer, 43 dBA
This dot-matrix printer has the following features:
- A 9-pin print head
- A maximum speed of 270 characters per second in draft mode, and 40 characters per second in letter quality (LQ) mode.
- Eight built-in fonts.
- 8K of RAM for a print buffer.
- A noise level rating of 43 decibels.

To help you identify the type of printer that's best for you, use the following printer checklist.

Printer checklist

Print speed: ____ pages per minute (PPM)   — laser printers

____ characters per second (cps)   — inkjet/dot-matrix printers (draft mode)

____ characters per second (cps)   — inkjet and dot-matrix printers (letter quality mode)

Print resolution: ❏ 600 dpi   ❏ 400 dpi
❏ 360 dpi   ❏ 300 dpi
____ dpi

Number of built-in fonts: _____

Built-in RAM: _____ Kilobytes or Megabytes

Printer emulation: ❏ Hewlett-Packard laser printers   ❏ Epson dot-matrix printers
❏ Other _____

Interfaces available: ❑ Parallel port   ❑ Serial port
                          ❑ AppleTalk   ❑ Network

Automatic Interface Switching: ❑ Yes   ❑ No

Footprint: _____ width   _____ height
                _____ depth

Power-saving feature: ❑ Yes   ❑ No
(Applicable for laser printers only)

Warranty: ❑ 3 Year   ❑ 2 Year
               ❑ 1 Year   ❑ 30 Days

Dealer:

_____

Price:

_____

"Green" printers

From a "green" point of view, the most energy-efficient printers are inkjet and dot-matrix printers because they consume relatively little electricity when not in use. To meet the Energy Star requirements, a laser printer must reduce power consumption to less than 30 watts when not in use.

The following lists several "green" laser printer manufacturers:

Brother Laser Printer HL-6, HL-10h
Brother International Corporation
200 Cottontail Lane
Somerset, NJ 08875-6714
Tel: (908) 356-8880
Fax: (908) 356-4085

Green Rating: *
(One star for energy-saving features)

Canon LBP-430
Canon Computer Systems, Inc.
2995 Redhill Avenue
Costa Mesa, CA 92626
Tel: (800) 848-4123
Fax: (714) 438-3099

Green Rating: **
(One star for energy-saving features)
(One star for toner recycling program)

Comments: Besides meeting the Energy Star requirements, Canon also offers a toner recycling program called Canon's Clean Earth Campaign. Whenever your toner cartridge runs out, just send it back to Canon and they'll recycle it for you. Through Canon's Clean Earth Campaign, toner cartridges will get reused instead of dumped in a landfill.

Epson ActionLaser 1000
Epson America Inc.
20770 Madrona Avenue
Torrance, CA 90509-2842
Tel: (310) 782-0770
Fax: (310) 782-4248

Green Rating: *
(One star for energy-saving features)

Hewlett-Packard LaserJet 4L, 4ML
Hewlett-Packard Company
P.O. Box 58059
MS511L-SJ
Santa Clara, CA 95051-8059
Tel: (800) 752-0900
Fax: (800) 333-1917

Green Rating: **
(One star for energy-saving
features)
(One star for toner cartridge
recycling)

Comments: Hewlett-Packard's laser printers consume up to 5 watts of power when not in use, the lowest among all laser printers. In addition, Hewlett-Packard now sells remanufactured toner cartridges under the Optiva label.

Kyocera Ecosys
Kyocera 100 Randolph Road
Somerset, NJ 08875
Tel: (908) 560-3400
Fax: (908) 560-8380

Green Rating: **
(One star for energy-saving features)
(One star for eliminating throwaway
items)

Comments: Most laser printers use printer drums that wear out or toner cartridges that need replacing. Both of these items commonly find their way into landfills. To avoid this problem, the Kyocera Ecosys laser printers use a printer drum designed to last the life of the printer and eliminates the need for toner cartridges altogether. Instead of using toner cartridges, the Kyocera Ecosys printers just require you to pour in toner once in a while.

Lexmark IBM 4039 10R
Lexmark International, Inc.
740 New Circle Road
Lexington, KY 40511-1847
Tel: (606) 232-2000
Fax: (606) 232-5439

Green Rating: **
(One star for energy-saving features)
(One star for toner cartridge
recycling)

Comments: Lexmark, a former division of IBM, still makes printers and keyboards for IBM. Besides selling laser printers that meet the Energy Star requirements, Lexmark also offers a toner cartridge recycling program called Operation ReSource. Whenever your toner cartridge runs out, just send it back to Lexmark and they'll recycle it for you. Through Operation ReSource, toner cartridges will get reused instead of dumped in a landfill.

NEC Silentwriter SuperScript 610
NEC Technologies, Inc.
1414 Massachusetts Avenue
Boxborough, MA 01719
Tel: (508) 264-8000
Fax: (508) 264-8265

Green Rating: *
(One star for energy-saving features)

Okidata OL400e
Okidata
532 Fellowship Road
Mt. Laurel, NJ 08054
Tel: (609) 235-2600
Fax: (609) 778-4184

Green Rating: *
(One star for energy-saving features)

Panasonic KX-P4440
Panasonic SideWriter KX-P5400
Panasonic Communications
& Systems Company
Two Panasonic Way
Secaucus, NJ 07094
Tel: (800) 742-8086
Fax: (201) 392-4500

Green Rating: *
(One star for energy-saving features)

Sharp JX-9400
Sharp Electronics Corporation
Sharp Plaza
Mahwah, NJ 07430
Tel: (201) 529-9593
Fax: (201) 529-9637

Green Rating: *
(One star for energy-saving features)

TI MicroLaser Pro 600
Texas Instruments, Inc.
P.O. Box 200230
Austin, TX 78720
Tel: (817) 771-5856
Fax: (817) 774-6751

Green Rating: *
(One star for energy-saving features)

14
Shopping for parts

Once you've decided on the types of parts you want to use in your "green" PC, the next step is to buy these parts at the lowest price possible, with the least amount of risk. Basically, there are three different places to buy computer parts:

- Direct from the manufacturer
- Mail-order
- Local dealers

Buying direct from the manufacturer should be your last resort if you absolutely cannot find a part anywhere else. Many of the larger manufacturers of monitors and motherboards won't even sell direct to individuals, and when they do, they'll usually charge the normal (high) retail price for their products.

Mail-order dealers can be found in magazines like *Computer Shopper*, *PC Magazine*, and *PC World*. These dealers usually sell products at 30% to 60% off the retail price. If you order from an out-of-state dealer, you won't have to pay sales tax either. For a $1,000 purchase, avoiding a state sales tax of 7% would save you $70. If you bought all of your computer parts out-of-state, avoiding sales tax can add up to a substantial amount of money.

Unfortunately, mail-order also entails the biggest risk. Horror stories abound of mail-order dealers who deliberately deceive customers, either shipping inferior or defective products or not shipping products at all, and then skipping out with the customer's money.

Although fraudulent mail-order dealers do exist, most of them have been weeded out. For safety, most people order with a credit card, which gives them the option of removing the charges if they don't receive their merchandise within a reasonable amount of time.

More common problems with mail-order dealers include lost or damaged merchandise along with the long wait between the time you order your product and the time it actually arrives at your door. Even worse, if you have problems with your product or find that you ordered the wrong item, returning that item and getting a refund or replacement is time-consuming and inconvenient.

But despite these possible problems, mail-order dealers are popular because they offer such steep discounts on products, offer a wider variety of products than local dealers, and often include toll-free technical support hotlines in case you have a problem with their merchandise. Once you find a reputable mail-order dealer that you trust, you'll find that ordering products can be easier and cheaper than buying from a local dealer.

Yet no matter how attractive mail-order dealers may be, many people still prefer to shop from local dealers instead. Even then, there are three types of local dealers to choose from:

- Computer franchises
- Specialized computer dealers
- Swap meets

Computer franchises usually sell equipment made by name brand companies like IBM, Intel, Epson, Mitsubishi, NCR, Packard Bell, and Zenith. Naturally, name brand equipment is usually more expensive than lesser known but equivalent brands, but name brand parts offer warranties that will be honored across the country. A computer franchise is usually geared more for people who want a computer but don't want to fix or build it themselves, but specialized computer dealers are more apt to sell no-name computers and generic parts that work just as well as name brand equipment. Often, specialized computer dealers will offer steep discounts on all their merchandise, sometimes rivaling or surpassing mail-order dealer prices. Best of all, you can examine your equipment before you buy it, something impossible to do with mail-order dealers. If you have a problem, you can call or visit your local dealer whenever you need help.

Computer swap meets are usually organized by local dealers or computer user groups. The main advantage of these swap meets is that you can find equipment at extremely low prices. Because these parts are usually sold by local dealers in the area, you get all the advantage of buying from a local dealer while saving more money than you could by buying through mail-order. Unfortunately, swap meets can be wildly unpredictable. Sometimes you may not be able to find the type of hard disk you need. Other times you won't be able to buy the monitor you want. Swap meets may offer the lowest prices available, but you may not always find what you're looking for when you need it.

Where to shop

Most major cities have plenty of local dealers around who would be happy to sell you individual computer parts and give advice on putting it together. But if you don't have a local dealer around or if you prefer to do your shopping by mail-order, here's a short list of sources where you can find mail-order dealers.

Magazines

Nearly every computer magazine will contain advertisements or classified ads that offer computer equipment and software. However, the following three magazines specifically target readers who are interested in building or upgrading their computers by themselves.

BYTE
One Phoenix Mill Lane
Peterborough, NH 03458
Tel: (800) 257-9402

Comments: Each issue of this monthly magazine combines reviews and product comparisons along with feature articles on new technology other computer-related issues. Because *BYTE* caters to more technically-inclined audiences, you'll find plenty of advertisements selling different types of computer parts for building your own computer or upgrading an existing one.

Computer Shopper
One Park Avenue, 11th Floor
New York, NY 10016
Tel: (800) 274-6384

Comments: Each issue of this monthly magazine comes packed with over 700 pages of articles, reviews, and advertisements for buying, using, and modifying computer equipment. If you're looking for a mail-order dealer, this is the magazine to buy.

Besides providing a huge number of mail-order advertisements, *Computer Shopper* also provides a customer service representative. If you have any complaints or problems with any mail-order dealer advertising in *Computer Shopper*, the magazine will intervene and help you. *Computer Shopper* has been known to refuse advertising from any mail-order dealer who consistently cheats or deceives customers.

PC Magazine
P.O. Box 54093
Boulder, CO 80322-4093
Tel: (800) 289-0429

Comments: This biweekly magazine comes jam-packed with both hardware and software reviews of a variety of products. Their annual printer issue is an exhaustive review of every type of printer imaginable. If you want to keep up with the latest technological advances in the computer industry, this is the magazine to read.

PC Upgrade
KableNews/Publisher's Aide
308 East Hitt Street
Mt. Morris, IL 61054
Tel: (800) 877-5487

Comments: This bimonthly magazine contains articles and advertisements geared towards upgrading and building an IBM-compatible computer. Many articles provide step-by-step installation guides for installing your own hard disk, CD-ROM drive, or tape backup unit. Each issue also includes a calendar listing all the computer swap meets for the upcoming three months.

Windows Upgrade
600 Community Drive
Manhasset, NY 11030
Tel: (800) 284-3584

Comments: This monthly magazine contains articles and advertisements geared towards upgrading or building an IBM computer specifically to run Microsoft Windows.

Like *PC Upgrade Magazine*, *Windows Upgrade* also includes articles that provides step-by-step instructions for installing memory chips, hard disks, or network cards.

Computer conventions and trade shows

Each year, the computer industry attends several trade shows in different parts of the world. No matter where you may live, each year you should be able to find at least one convention close by.

The most attended computer convention in the United States is COMDEX, organized by The Interface Group. The Fall COMDEX show is held every November in Las Vegas. The Spring version of COMDEX is usually held in a Midwest city, like Atlanta or Chicago, but isn't as highly attended as the Fall COMDEX in Las Vegas.

Because many companies introduce new products at these trade shows, you can often find and buy equipment not yet available anywhere else. At the very least, you'll meet more manufacturers, dealers, and software publishers at one show than you could possibly ever contact by yourself in one day. Call The Interface Group for show schedules, locations, and admission prices.

The Interface Group
300 First Avenue
Needham, MA 02194-2722
Tel: (617) 449-6600
Fax: (617) 444-0165

On-line services

In case you don't have access to any local dealers, you can get plenty of free help and advice from any number of on-line services. Just post a message describing your problem, and half a dozen (or more) people will gladly provide you with the information you need, or at least guide you in the direction where you can find an answer to your question.

To entice new subscribers, most on-line services offer an introductory offer where you can try their service for free for a limited amount of time. If you decide to subscribe, the on-line service will bill your credit card a flat-fee every month plus charges per minute each time you use the on-line service. If you're not careful, an on-line service can get very expensive.

America Online
American Online, Inc.
8619 Westwood Center Drive, #200
Vienna, VA 22182-2285
Tel: (800) 827-6364
Fax: (703) 883-1509

Comments: America Online is one of the easiest on-line services to use because it comes with its own communications program that makes using this service almost effortless. Like all on-line services, America Online has plenty of files for downloading, business and financial news, and research databases to explore.

CompuServe Information Service
CompuServe, Inc.
P.O. Box 20212
Columbus, OH 43220
Tel: (800) 848-8199
Fax: (614) 457-0802

Comments: CompuServe is the granddaddy of the on-line services and also the most expensive. For the price though, you get the largest selection of files for downloading, access to numerous special-interest groups to join, online shopping malls, financial and business news, and the largest number of research databases of all the online services. Best of all, CompuServe supports baud rates up to 14,400 bps. The other on-line services only support the slower 2400 or 9600 baud rates.

Delphi
General Videotex Corporation
1030 Massachusetts Avenue
Cambridge, MA 02138
Tel: (800) 695-4005
Fax: (617) 491-6642

Comments: Delphi is one of the smallest and least expensive on-line services available. However, it's the only on-line service that offers full access to the Internet, unlike other on-line services which only offer access to Internet mail. If you want Internet access, Delphi is the least expensive option. But if you want anything else, Delphi is too small and limited compared to the other competing on-line services.

GEnie
GEnie Service
401 N. Washington Street
Rockville, MD 20850
Tel: (800) 638-9636
Fax: (301) 251-6421

Comments: GEnie is one of the least expensive on-line services but also one of the more comprehensive. Many people use GEnie as a low-cost alternative to CompuServe, because GEnie offers many of the same types of services.

Prodigy Interactive Personal Service
Prodigy Services Co.
445 Hamilton Avenue
White Plains, NY 10601
Tel: (800) 776-3449
Fax: (914) 993-8000

Comments: Prodigy is geared mostly for home and personal use, as compared to business use that the other on-line services specialize in. As a result, Prodigy places less emphasis on downloading files and electronic mail and more emphasis on flashy graphics, news reports, and illustrated editions of *National Geographic*. For children, Prodigy will be the most appealing and useful.

Besides these commercial on-line services, you can also find plenty of local electronic bulletin board systems (BBSs) in nearly every city in America. A BBS is essentially a personal computer and a modem that somebody has connected to a phone line. Anyone can call them. Some charge a fee while others are absolutely free.

Once you're connected to a BBS, you can copy programs or trade messages with other people. Many of the more active BBSs have plenty of callers who will be able to help with any problems you might have with your computer. To find a list of BBSs near you, look in *Computer Shopper* or *Boardwatch Magazine*, which regularly prints a nationwide list organized by area code.

Mail-order dealers

The number of mail-order companies keeps growing, so no matter what you're looking for, you can find a mail-order dealer who can sell it to you. Although price can be a major factor in choosing a mail-order dealer, ecologically minded consumers might prefer supporting mail-order companies that actively engage in recycling or environmental causes.

By spending most of your money with ecologically minded companies, you'll not only be buying "green" parts and equipment, but you'll also be supporting companies that practice "green" policies as well.

ErgoSource
2828 Hedberg Drive
Minnetonka, MN 55305
Tel: (612) 595-0881
Fax: (612) 595-0884

Green Rating: *
(One star for specializing in ergonomic furniture and accessories)

Comments: ErgoSource sells ergonomically designed computer desks, chairs, wrist supports, arm rests, monitor stands, foot rests, and hand tools. In addition, this company also sells books and videotapes on how to reduce the risk of injury while working. If you're looking for an item to make your work area safe and comfortable, ErgoSource probably sells it.

Evergreen Computer Systems
661 G Street
Arcata, CA 95521
Tel: (707) 826-7476
Fax: (707) 826-7480

Green Rating: *
(One star for belonging to Co-op America's Association of Socially Responsible Enterprises and Business Partnership for Peace)

Comments: Evergreen Computer Systems sells complete Energy Star-compliant computers along with Energy Star monitors and printers. In addition, you can also buy software, memory chips, and other types of parts necessary for building your own computer.

Real Goods
966 Mazzoni Street
Ukiah, CA 95482-3471
Tel: (800) 762-7325
Fax: (707) 468-9486

Green Rating: *
(One star for using recycled paper and selling ecologically friendly products)

Comments: Real Goods sells shields to reduce your monitor's electromagnetic emissions and hand-held monitors to measure excessive radiation. For those tinkerers who want to protect the environment in other ways, Real Goods sells solar panels, air purifiers, organic cleaning solutions, and energy-conserving light bulbs.

PC Connection
14 Mill Street
Marlow, NH 03456
Tel: (603) 446-7711
Fax: (603) 446-7791

Green Rating: *
(One star for in-house recycling programs)

Comments: One of the most ecologically minded mail-order dealers in the business is PC Connection, which has been in business since 1984. Besides selling products at discounts between 20% and 40% off retail price, PC Connection also has several in-house recycling programs.

One program recycles all the waste paper that the employees toss out, and converts this waste paper into packaging material for shipping out products. A second program takes all the waste food from the company's cafeteria and turns it into a compost heap for use in the gardens surrounding the company. Employees are also free to take this compost for their own use.

Although PC Connection doesn't sell motherboards, cases, or power supplies, they do sell most everything else you need to build your own computer including monitors, memory chips, printers, and software. If you want to support a "green" mail-order company, PC Connection is the one to choose.

Self Care
5850 Shellmound Street
Emeryville, CA 94662-0813
Tel: (800) 345-3371
Fax: (800) 345-4021

Green Rating: *
(One star for selling ergonomically designed health care products)

Comments: Self Care sells back supports, seat cushions, and wrist braces to maximize your comfort while you are sitting in front of your computer. Other products sold by Self Care include natural vitamin pills, biofeedback meters, and exercise equipment.

Shopping recommendations

One of the biggest problems that can occur when building your own PC is that the motherboard and power supply don't fit inside the computer case you bought. Because motherboards and power supplies come in different sizes and shapes, it's possible to buy parts that simply won't fit inside your computer case. To avoid this problem, buy all these parts from one dealer, who can make sure that everything fits together before you get it.

Another possible problem might occur when you buy a hard drive and a hard drive controller card. Some motherboards have a built-in IDE controller card, while some hard disks come with an IDE controller card as part of the price. Even worse, some hard disks require a SCSI controller instead of an IDE controller. To avoid winding up with two IDE controller cards or the wrong type of hard disk controller card, it's also a good idea to buy the IDE controller card and the hard disk from the same dealer.

Ideally, you should only buy parts from dealers where you can return your merchandise or get a refund altogether. Most mail-order dealers offer a standard 30-day money-back guarantee, and most local dealers offer some refund policy as well. The more support you can get from your dealer, the easier it will be to build your own "green" PC.

15
Putting it together

Once you've bought all the parts that you need, the final step involves putting it all together. Fortunately, computers are designed to be taken apart easily, so putting one together only requires snapping or screwing pieces together and connecting cables.

Building a computer can take anywhere from 45 minutes to a few hours, depending on your technical skill and familiarity with computers. But no matter how long it may take, be patient. Half the fun of building your own computer comes from seeing how all the parts work together. The other half of the fun comes in using a computer you put together with your own hands.

Choose an operating system

An operating system controls your computer and determines the types of programs you can run. Once you finish building your computer, you'll need an operating system to make it work. Four of the most popular operating systems to choose from are:

- MS-DOS
- PC-DOS
- Novell DOS
- Windows

Because MS-DOS has been the standard for IBM-compatible computers ever since IBM introduced it in 1981, most people choose MS-DOS for guaranteed compatibility and reliability. As an alternative to MS-DOS, IBM introduced its own version called PC-DOS. Essentially, PC-DOS is a repackaged version of MS-DOS with slightly different utility programs included. For example, MS-DOS uses a subset of Central Point's anti-virus program while PC-DOS uses IBM's own anti-virus program that can catch more viruses than MS-DOS. Because PC-DOS is essentially MS-DOS, PC-DOS is just as reliable and compatible as MS-DOS.

The third operating system is Novell DOS, originally called DR DOS. The main advantage of Novell DOS is that it includes support for networks. If you want to create an inexpensive network, then Novell DOS is your only choice.

But be careful. Because Novell DOS is not based on MS-DOS, Microsoft programs, like Windows, may not work with Novell DOS. When Microsoft introduced Windows 3.1, they made sure it only worked with MS-DOS or PC-DOS. If you can live with possible incompatibilities with Microsoft software, then Novell DOS may be your best choice.

If you're planning on running Microsoft Windows 3.1, you'll need a copy of MS-DOS, PC-DOS, or Novell DOS. But if you want to run Windows 4.0 and later, you won't need a copy of MS-DOS at all.

Before you start: safety first

Building your own computer is not difficult, but to reduce the possibility of problems, make sure of the following:

- Do you have all the tools you need?
- Are all parts intact and appear to be in working order?
- Do you have all the parts you need to build your computer?
- Do you have a large, clean work area?
- Is there enough light so you can see easily?
- Are there enough electrical outlets?
- Have you grounded yourself to prevent static electricity?

The only types of tools you'll need are a flathead screwdriver, a Phillips screwdriver, needle-nose pliers, and a small flashlight for peering into small places. As a precaution, you might want to invest in an anti-static wrist band or mat as well.

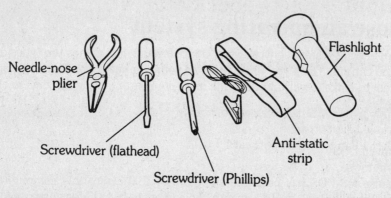

Needle-nose plier

Flashlight

Screwdriver (flathead)

Screwdriver (Phillips)

Anti-static strip

15-1 The necessary tools for building your own computer.

Collect all the manuals that came with your motherboard, video adapter card, CD-ROM drive, sound card, etc. Don't be surprised to find that most computer manuals are poorly designed, written, and organized. If you can understand one-tenth of what the manual's trying to tell you, consider yourself lucky.

Computer manuals tend to look like a sixth-generation photocopy of instructions that nobody bothered to verify. For example, my CD-ROM drive manual contained three pages of instructions for getting the CD-ROM drive to work with the computer.

After bombarding you with three pages of small print instructions, the final step said, "Warning! Do not follow these steps if you are running MS-DOS 3.3 or higher. If you are running MS-DOS 3.3 or higher, refer to section 8.4 for more information."

Unfortunately, the manual was only divided into seven sections so section 8.4 existed only in the manual writer's imagination. Secondly, why was the warning placed at the end of the instruction steps, especially because nearly everyone these days is running MS-DOS 3.3 or higher? If you feel frustrated, helpless, and angry after following so-called "instructions," rest assured that you are not alone.

In the event that you lack a knowledgeable computer guru who you can bribe to help you with any problems, don't be afraid to take your computer to a technician for help. Even with the added labor charges, you'll still wind up saving more money than if you bought a computer already built by somebody else.

Step 1. Make sure you have all the parts you need

Once you've bought all the parts you need to build your computer, inspect them for visible damage like cracks or bends. Keep all the parts packaged in their original containers, and use the following checklist to make sure you have all the parts that you need:

Computer parts checklist

- Motherboard
- Microprocessor (CPU)
- Random access memory chips (RAM)
- Floppy drive(s)
- Hard drive
- Floppy drive/Hard drive controller card
- Video adapter card
- Serial/Parallel/Game port card
- Monitor
- Case
- Power supply
- Keyboard
- Mouse
- Your operating system disks (MS-DOS, PC-DOS, Novell DOS, OS/2, Windows)

Depending on the types of parts you've bought, you may not need all of these items. For example, your motherboard may have serial or parallel ports built-in, so you won't need a separate serial/parallel/game port card. Likewise, your keyboard may have an integrated trackball or other pointing device, so you won't need a separate mouse.

Step 2. Check your work area

Your work area should be spacious enough to lay all your computer parts out where you can see them, and still give you enough room to put pieces together. Make sure you have plenty of lighting so you can see what you're doing, and make sure you have enough electrical outlets as well. Don't overload an electric outlet by plugging in too many items, and always turn off any item before plugging it in.

Step 3. Ground yourself

Before you touch any of your computer parts, ground yourself first to discharge any static electricity. You can ground yourself by touching any metal item nearby, like a lamp or chair, or you can buy a special anti-static wrist band or pad. If you fail to ground yourself, any static electricity can "fry" an electronic part in a second. More than one careless technician has been known to wreck a $500 microprocessor through static electricity, so make sure you're grounded before touching any of your computer parts.

Step 4. Install the power supply into the case

The power supply fits in the back corner of the computer case. The back of the power supply contains a fan and electrical outlets that stick out through the back of your computer case. Simply slide the power supply in the corner of the computer case and tighten the screws in the back of the power supply to secure it to the back of the computer case.

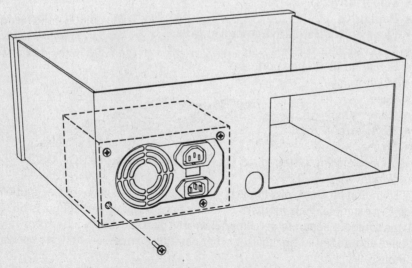

15-2 Screws to tighten in the power supply.

Step 5. Install the motherboard into the computer case

The motherboard fits into your computer case with the expansion slots flush against the expansion slot openings in the back of the computer case. To secure your motherboard to the computer case, your computer case comes with several holes in the bottom.

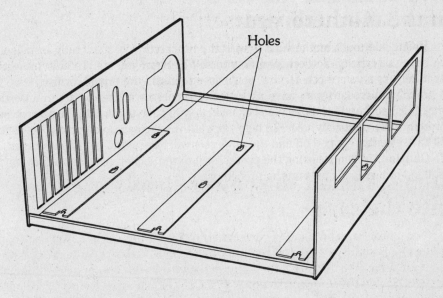

Holes

15-3 Holes in the bottom of the computer case.

Your motherboard comes with several plastic or metal objects called standoffs. Insert these standoffs through the holes in the bottom of the computer case. Then align the motherboard so the standoffs poke through the holes in the motherboard.

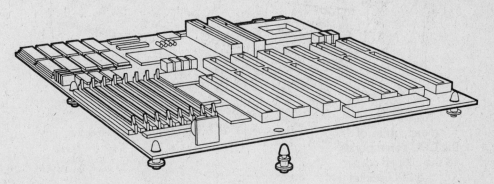

15-4 Standoffs in the motherboard.

Once you've placed the motherboard over the standoffs, fill the remaining holes with screws to secure the motherboard in place. Depending on your motherboard, you may need anywhere from two to four screws.

Your motherboard will also have several connections for your computer's speaker, reset switch, and LEDs on the front panel. Refer to your motherboard's manual for connecting these wires from your motherboard to your computer case.

Step 6. Install the CPU in the motherboard

Most dealers sell motherboards with the processor (CPU) already installed. If you have this type of motherboard, skip to step 6. But if you bought your processor separately from your motherboard, you'll have to install the processor first.

Your motherboard may have an ordinary processor socket or a zero-insertion force (ZIF) socket. With both types of sockets, you have to align the processor pins correctly with the socket holes. To help you put the processor in correctly, the socket will have a corner clipped off and the processor will have a tiny dot in one corner.

Caution: When inserting the processor into the socket, make sure that you do not bend or break any pins on the processor.

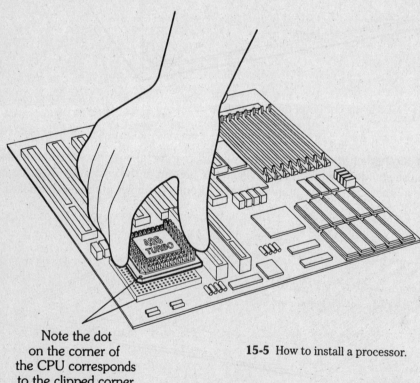

Note the dot on the corner of the CPU corresponds to the clipped corner of the CPU socket

15-5 How to install a processor.

Align the dot on the processor with the clipped corner of the processor socket. If your motherboard has a ZIF socket, then drop the processor in the socket and pull the ZIF lever down to hold or "lock" the processor in place. Because the ZIF socket must firmly hold the processor in place, you may have to push the lever fairly hard. If your motherboard has an ordinary socket, then gently guide the processor in place and press firmly.

Step 7. Install the memory chips in the motherboard

Many motherboards already have memory chips installed. If you have this type of motherboard, skip to step 7. But if you bought your memory chips separately from your motherboard, you'll have to install the memory next.

Most computers use SIMMs, which look like little circuit cards. The SIMM sockets on the motherboard are usually white. To make sure you install a SIMM correctly, SIMMs have a tiny notch cut out from one corner. If you examine the SIMM sockets on the motherboard, you'll find that the notched end of the SIMM can only fit in the socket one way.

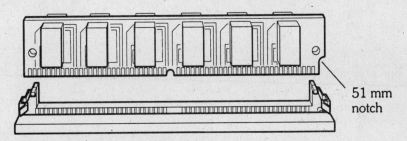

51 mm notch

15-6 A SIMM notch and SIMM socket.

To install a SIMM, gently insert each SIMM into a memory socket at approximately a 45-degree angle. Then pull it upright until the retaining arms snap over the edge of the SIMM, holding it in place.

Step 8. Connect the power supply to the motherboard

The power supply is a big metal box with all sorts of colorful wires sticking out of it. At the end of each wire are plastic plugs. Look for two plugs labeled P8 and P9. These plugs plug into your motherboard's power supply connector.

The shape of the power supply plugs prevents you from plugging them in the wrong way. To make sure you plug them in the right position, make sure the four black wires are in the center.

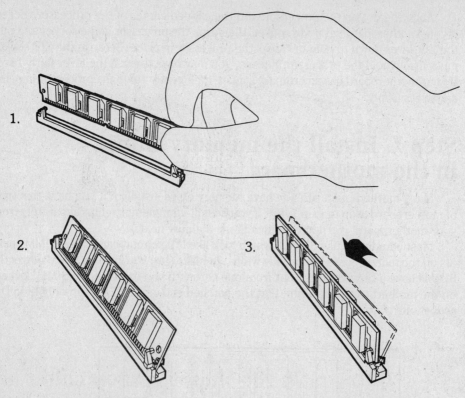

1.

2.   3.

15-7 How to install a SIMM.

15-8 The shape
of a power
supply plug.

Note the four black
wires in the center

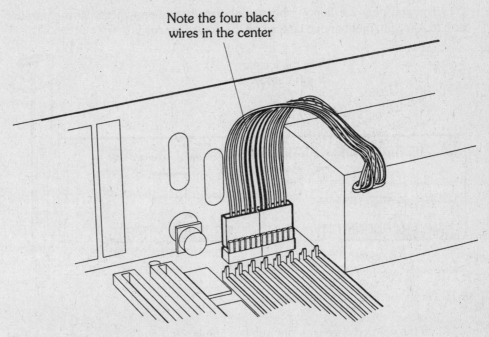

15-9 The four black wires in the center.

Step 9. Connect the floppy ribbon cable to the floppy/hard drive controller card

The floppy ribbon cable is the one that has part of it cut out and twisted. One edge of the floppy ribbon cable will have a colored wire. The colored wire signifies pin number one.

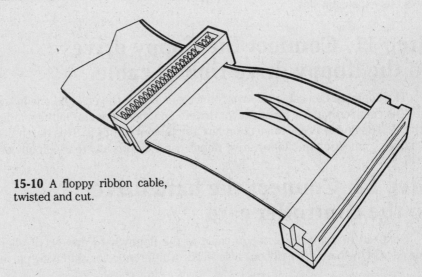

15-10 A floppy ribbon cable,
twisted and cut.

When you plug the floppy ribbon cable into your floppy/hard drive controller card, look for pin number one labeled on the controller card.

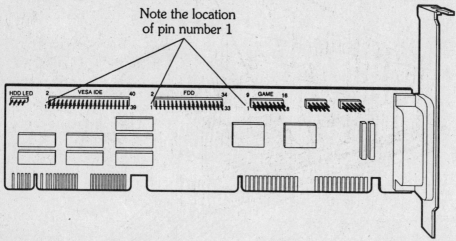

15-11 Pin number one on the controller card.

Align the colored wire with pin number one labeled on the controller card. Doing this ensures that you plug the ribbon cable in the controller card correctly.

Step 10. Plug in the floppy/hard drive controller card

Plug in your floppy/hard drive controller card in any open expansion slot. Some controller cards plug into an ISA expansion slot, while some plug into a VESA or PCI local bus expansion slot.

Step 11. Connect the floppy drives to the floppy drive ribbon cable

The floppy ribbon cable has two connectors: one at the end and one in the middle. The connector at the far end is for drive A and the connector in the middle is for drive B. The floppy drive connection has a notch cut out of it. This notch prevents you from connecting the floppy drive ribbon cable incorrectly to the floppy drive.

Step 12. Connect the hard drive to the controller card

Connect the hard drive ribbon cable to the floppy/hard drive controller card. One edge of the hard drive ribbon cable will be a different color, signifying pin number

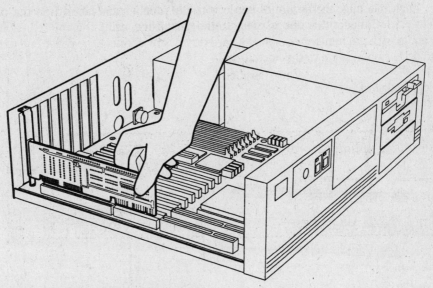

15-12 How to install an expansion card.

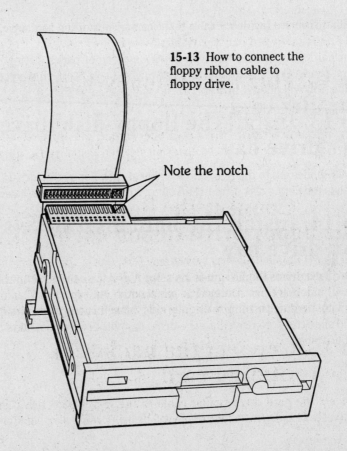

15-13 How to connect the floppy ribbon cable to floppy drive.

Note the notch

one. Align this edge of the ribbon cable with pin number one labeled on the controller card. Connect this ribbon cable to the hard drive, using the colored edge to match up with pin number one on the hard drive. Now connect the other end of the hard drive ribbon cable to the hard drive.

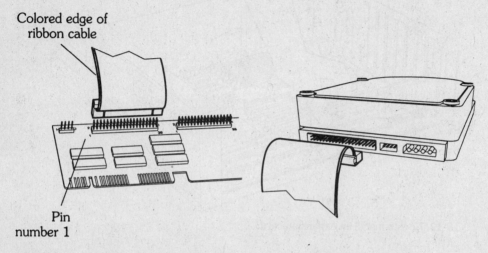

15-14 How to connect the ribbon cable to the controller card and hard drive.

Your hard drive should have come with a piece of paper, listing the number of cylinders, heads, tracks, etc. that the hard drive uses. Store this piece of paper in a safe place. You will need it in step 16.

Step 13. Install the floppy disk drive(s) into a drive bay

Attach guide rails to the right and left side of each floppy disk drive. The guide rails let you slide the floppy disk drive in and out of a drive bay and holds it securely in place.

Step 14. Install the hard disk drive(s) into a drive bay

Some hard drives require guide rails like floppy disk drives. Other hard drives fit snugly within a drive bay. Determine which drive bay you want to install the hard disk. If your hard drive requires guide rails, attach them to each side of the hard drive and slide the hard drive into the drive bay. Otherwise, just slide the hard drive into the drive bay.

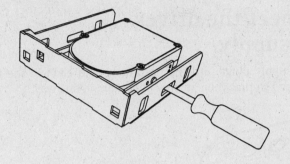

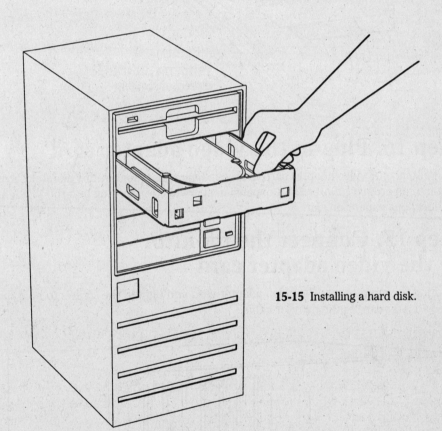

15-15 Installing a hard disk.

Step 15. Connect the drives
to the power supply

Connect the power supply plugs into the hard drive and each of the floppy drives. The plugs are shaped so that you can only plug them in one way.

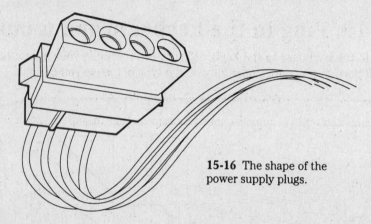

15-16 The shape of the power supply plugs.

Step 16. Plug in the video adapter card

Plug in your video adapter card in an expansion slot. Some video adapter cards plug into an ordinary ISA or EISA expansion slot while others plug into the VESA or PCI local bus expansion slot.

Step 17. Connect the monitor
to the video adapter card

Plug the monitor into the video adapter card and tighten the screws to hold the video adapter card to the monitor cable.

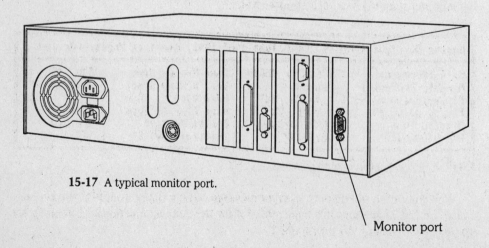

15-17 A typical monitor port.

Monitor port

Step 18. Plug in the serial/parallel/game port card

Plug in your serial/parallel/game port card in any open expansion slot and tighten the screws to hold the card to the computer case.

Step 19. Plug in the keyboard and mouse

Plug in the keyboard to the keyboard connector. Plug in your mouse to a serial port, PS/2 port, or bus port, depending on the type of mouse you bought.

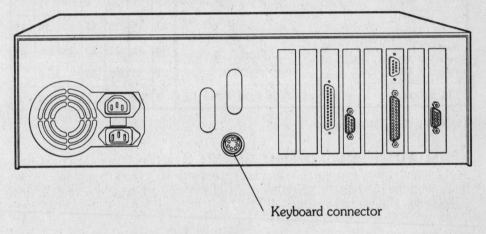

Keyboard connector

15-18 The location of the keyboard connector.

Step 20. Test the computer

Turn on the computer and the monitor. If everything is working correctly, your computer should display the manufacturer's name and date of the BIOS along with the amount of memory your computer has.

```
System Configuration (C) Copyright 1985-1992, American Megatrends Inc,.

Main Processor      : 486DX or 486SX    Base Memory Size    : 640  KB
Numeric Processor   : Present            Ext. Memory Size    : 7424 KB
Floppy Drive A:     : 1.44 MB, 3½"       Hard Disk C: Type   : 47
Floppy Drive B:     : 1.2 MB, 5¼"        Hard Disk D: Type   : None
Display Type        : VGA/PGA/EGA        Serial Port(s)      : 3F8,2F8
ROM-BIOS Date       : 06/13/92           Parallel Port(s)    : 378
```

15-19 A typical boot-up opening screen.

The computer will display an error message, saying that it couldn't continue because the CMOS settings are incorrect. Follow the instructions on the screen to set up the CMOS, usually by pressing F1.

```
┌─────────────────────────────────────────────────────────────────────┐
│        CMOS SETUP (C) Copyright 1985-1992, American Megatrends Inc,.  │
├──────────────────────────────────────┬────────────────────────────────┤
│ Date (mn/date/year): Wed, Mar 02 1994 │ Base Memory Size    : 640  KB  │
│ Time (hour/min/sec): 15 : 06 : 33     │ Ext. Memory Size    : 7424 KB  │
│ Floppy Drive A:     : 1.44 MB, 3½"    │ Numeric processor   : Present  │
│ Floppy Drive B:     : 1.2 MB, 5¼"     │                                │
│                                       │ Cyln Head WPcom LZone Sec Size │
│ Hard disk C: type   : 47 = USER TYPE  │ 1011  15    0   1011   44 326 MB│
│ Hard disk D: type   : Not Installed   │                                │
│ Primary display     : VGA/PGA/EGA     ├────┬───┬───┬───┬───┬───┬────┤
│ Keyboard            : Installed       │Sun │Mon│Tue│Wed│Thu│Fri│Sat │
│                                       ├────┼───┼───┼───┼───┼───┼────┤
│ Scratch RAM option : 1                │ 27 │28 │ 1 │ 2 │ 3 │ 4 │ 5  │
│ Main BIOS shadow   : Enabled          ├────┼───┼───┼───┼───┼───┼────┤
│                                       │  6 │ 7 │ 8 │ 9 │10 │11 │12  │
│                                       ├────┼───┼───┼───┼───┼───┼────┤
│                                       │ 13 │14 │15 │16 │17 │18 │19  │
├───────────────────────────────────────┼────┼───┼───┼───┼───┼───┼────┤
│ Month : Jan, Feb,.....Dec             │ 20 │21 │22 │23 │24 │25 │26  │
│ Date  : 01, 02, 03,...31              ├────┼───┼───┼───┼───┼───┼────┤
│ Year  : 1901, 1902,...2099            │ 27 │28 │29 │30 │31 │ 1 │ 2  │
├───────────────────────────────────────┼────┼───┼───┼───┼───┼───┼────┤
│ ESC = Exit,        = Select, PgUp/PgDn = Modify │ 3 │ 4 │ 5 │ 6 │ 7 │ 8 │ 9  │
└───────────────────────────────────────┴────┴───┴───┴───┴───┴───┴────┘
```

15-20 A typical CMOS screen.

The CMOS keeps track of the time, date, and the number of floppy and hard drives your computer has. Change the date, time, floppy drive A: and floppy drive B: settings. With the hard disk information you saved in step 10, type in your hard drive settings. Save your CMOS settings.

Step 21. Format your hard disk

1. Insert disk 1 of your operating system disk in drive A: and restart your computer by pressing the reset button, pressing Ctrl-Alt-Del, or shutting off the computer and turning it back on again.
2. When the A:> prompt appears, type FDISK and press Return. The FDISK options screen appears:

MS-DOS Version 6
Fixed Disk Setup Program
(C) Copyright Microsoft Corp. 1983 – 1993

FDISK Options

Current fixed disk drive: 1

Choose one of the following:

1. Create DOS partition or Logical DOS drive
2. Set active partition
3. Delete partition or Logical DOS drive
4. Display partition information

Enter choice: [1]

Press Esc to exit FDISK

    3. Type 1 to create a DOS partition. The Create DOS Partition or Logical DOS drive screen appears:

Create DOS partition or Logical DOS drive

Current fixed disk drive: 1

Choose one of the following:

1. Create Primary DOS Partition
2. Create Extended DOS Partition
3. Create Logical DOS Drive(s) in the Extended DOS Partition

Enter choice: [1]

Press Esc to exit FDISK Options

    4. Type 1 and press Return. The Create Primary DOS Partition screen appears:

                Create Primary DOS Partition

Current fixed disk drive: 1

Do you wish to use the maximum available size for a primary DOS partition and make the partition active?
(Y/N).........................?[Y]

Press Esc to return to FDISK Options

    5. Type Y and press Return. Press Esc several times until you exit out of the FDISK program and see the A:> prompt.
    6. Type FORMAT C:/S to format your hard disk. The computer will respond with a warning message:

WARNING! ALL DATA ON NONREMOVABLE DISK DRIVE C: WILL BE LOST!
                Proceed with Format (Y/N)

    7. Type Y. Your hard disk drive light should blink on and off as the computer formats it. When the computer is done, it will display a message like:

Format complete
System transferred
Volume label (11 characters, ENTER for none)?

    8. Type a name for your hard disk if you want. Then remove the operating system disk from drive A: and restart your computer by pressing the reset button, pressing Ctrl-Alt-Del, or turning the computer off and turning it on again. When the computer comes on again, you should see the C:> prompt.

Step 22. Install your operating system

Put disk 1 of your operating system in drive A: and run the SETUP program. Follow the instructions on the screen to install the operating system to your hard disk.

Step 23. Install your modem (optional)

If you have an internal modem, plug the modem into any open expansion slot. If you have an external modem, connect a serial cable to the modem and plug the cable into a serial port.

Step 24. Install sound card (optional)

If you have a sound card, follow the instructions for installing it in your computer.

Step 25. Install CD-ROM drive (optional)

Plug in the CD-ROM controller card into any open expansion slot. If you have an internal CD-ROM drive, connect the CD-ROM ribbon cable to the controller card, matching the colored edge of the ribbon cable with pin number one labeled on the controller card. Then connect the power supply plug into the CD-ROM drive. If you have an external CD-ROM drive, plug the CD-ROM drive into the port of the CD-ROM controller card.

Follow the instructions for installing the CD-ROM software on your computer. Once you have installed the software to control the CD-ROM drive, you will have to restart your computer again.

Step 26. Burn-in your computer

Electronic parts are highly reliable. However, if they do fail, they tend to fail within the first few times you use them. To detect faulty electronic parts, technicians test electronic equipment by leaving it turned on for 48 hours or more. This essentially torture-tests your equipment. If anything's going to fail, it's going to fail during this initial "burn-in" period when the parts are still covered by a warranty.

To burn-in your computer, leave it on for two days to two weeks straight. During this time, feel free to use your computer for playing games, word processing, or anything else you care to do with it. Just make sure you don't turn it off until the burn-in period is over. Once your computer passes its burn-in test, then turn it off whenever you're not using it.

16
Troubleshooting

In a perfect world, your computer will work from the time you put it together, and continue working perfectly from that point on. However, no matter what your technical skill or knowledge about computers may be, problems can always occur. Fortunately, most problems can be solved quickly and easily without resorting to expensive repairs. Some of the more common problems are caused by one or more of the following:

- Disconnected or loose cables
- Improperly installed expansion cards
- Improperly installed cable connectors
- Improper switch settings
- Dead or damaged equipment

As you're putting your computer together, make sure that you have connected all cables to their proper locations. When plugging cables, expansion cards, or memory chips into your computer, always make sure that you are not putting them in backwards, upside-down, etc. If any part refuses to plug together, don't force it. The plug's stubbornness may be the computer's way of telling you that you have the plug oriented the wrong way.

Caution: When troubleshooting your computer, always turn the power off before opening the case and probing around. Otherwise you may risk severe electrical shocks, which can ruin an otherwise perfectly good day.

Because defective computer parts are inevitable, make sure you save all your receipts for any equipment that you buy. Although manufacturers and distributors try to test all of their parts, there's still a chance you'll get a computer part that simply refuses to work because it was damaged during shipping or was defective from the start. If you save your receipts, you can always return the defective part for a new one, or get your money back.

When all else fails, assume that the part is defective and return it for a replacement part. If your replacement part also fails, then the problem is likely in another part of your computer. The following is a quick summary of common problems that might occur along with their simple solutions.

Startup failures

Every time you turn your computer on, it should display the following:
- The name of the BIOS manufacturer (like Phoenix, AMI, Award, etc.)
- The amount of memory the computer has
- The computer's CMOS information like the type of floppy disk drive designated as drive A:, the type of hard drive installed, etc.
- Any commands or programs listed in your computer's CONFIG.SYS or AUTOEXEC.BAT files

Problem:
The computer fails to turn on.

Solution:
1. Make sure the computer is plugged in. Also make sure that the cord from the electrical outlet to the computer is plugged in securely.
2. If the computer is plugged into a power strip, test the power strip to see if other items work when plugged in the power strip.
3. Make sure that the power supply is connected to the following items:
   A. The motherboard
   B. The floppy drives
   C. The hard drive
   D. The CD-ROM drive

Problem:
The computer turns on but nothing appears on the screen.

Solution:
1. Make sure the video card is plugged into the motherboard properly.
2. Make sure that the cable connecting the monitor to the video card is securely fastened.
3. Your monitor may be dead. Test it on another computer.

Problem:
The computer starts up but displays an error message on the screen and beeps.

Solution:
Your computer is trying to tell you that some part is defective. Instead of telling you in plain English that your motherboard may be bad, computers prefer displaying a cryptic error number instead like "101 Error." Table 16-1 lists some common error message numbers and what they mean:

Table 16-1. Common error messages and what they mean

Error number	What the problem is
101	Motherboard
201	Memory
301	Keyboard
401 or 501	Monitor or video adapter card
601	Floppy drive or controller card

701	Math coprocessor
901 or 1001	Parallel port
1101 or 1201	Serial port
1301	Game port or joystick
1401	Printer
1701	Hard drive or controller card

Problem:

Your computer displays the wrong date or time, "Invalid Setup" or "Configuration Error."

Solution:

1. The CMOS settings of your computer may be incorrect. Reboot the computer. Your computer should display a message like "Press F1 or <Del> to choose SETUP." Depending on which key your computer tells you to press, press either F1 or Del to display the CMOS setting screen so you can change the CMOS settings.
2. Your CMOS battery may be getting low. Replace the CMOS battery.

Hard, floppy, and CD-ROM drive failures

Each drive in your computer is designated by a letter. Usually floppy disk drives are designated as drive A: or drive B:. Hard drives are usually designated as drive C:, and CD-ROM drives can be designated anything from drive D: all the way to Z:

Problem:

The computer displays an "Invalid drive" error message.

Solution:

1. Check the CMOS settings to make sure that you have designated each floppy or hard drive properly. For example, if your drive A: is a 3.5-inch floppy drive but your CMOS settings think that drive A: is a 5.25-inch floppy drive, you'll get an error message.
2. CD-ROM drives usually come with an installation program. Run this program after making sure that all the cables are connected properly to the CD-ROM drive.

Problem:

The computer can't read files stored on a floppy disk.

Solution:

1. Make sure that the floppy disk has been formatted. A floppy drive cannot read an unformatted floppy disk.
2. Make sure the floppy disk is inserted in the floppy drive properly. Some floppy disks even have a latch that you need to close to hold the floppy disk securely in place.
3. The floppy disk may be defective or worn out. Floppy disks, like tape cassettes, eventually wear out after extended use. Try the floppy disk in another computer and save the files on a new floppy disk.

4. The files may have become damaged. Buy a special file utility program like The Norton Utilities or PC Tools that can attempt to save damaged files. If you are using MS-DOS 6.2, run the SCANDISK program by entering, for example, the following:

   SCANDISK A:

5. The floppy disk may be a high-density disk but your floppy drive is only a double-density drive.

6. If other computers can read the files off the floppy disk, you may have a defective floppy disk drive that needs replacing.

Problem:

Files have mysteriously disappeared or the computer can't read files stored on the hard disk.

Solution:

1. Make sure that the hard disk has been formatted.

2. The hard disk files may have been corrupted. Buy a special file utility program like The Norton Utilities or PC Tools that can attempt to save damaged files. If you are using MS-DOS 6.2, run the SCANDISK program like this:

   SCANDISK C:

3. Run the CHKDSK program to clean up any file fragments that are cluttering up your hard disk. Do so by entering:

   CHKDSK /F

Memory

Every computer needs memory, yet one bad memory chip can bring your whole computer crashing to its knees. Each time you turn on your computer, it checks that its memory chips exist, but it doesn't necessarily check to make sure they will all work.

Problem:

The computer displays a "201 Parity memory error" or something equally as cryptic.

Solution:

1. Make sure your memory chips are securely plugged into your motherboard.

2. You may have a bad memory chip. Either buy a replacement chip and exhaustively replace each old chip with the new one to find the defective chip, or take the easy way out and bring the whole computer to a repair shop and let them worry about it.

Problem:

The computer displays an "Out of memory" error message when you try to run a program, even though your computer is stuffed with plenty of memory.

Solution:

1. Run the MEM program to see how much memory your computer really has. Just type MEM at the DOS prompt. Many of the newer programs require several megabytes of memory to run, so if your computer has 4 megabytes

or less, it really may not have enough memory to run. In this case, you'll have to add more memory to your computer.

2. You may have too many programs already loaded using Windows or OS/2. Shut down one or two programs and try loading the program that caused the "Out of memory" error message.

3. If you get this message while running DOS, you may not have enough conventional memory, which is the first 640K of your computer's memory. If you have MS-DOS 6.0 or higher, run the MEMMAKER program, which will free up more conventional memory for DOS programs to use. Or buy a separate memory manager utility like QEMM, 386Max, or Netroom.

Monitors

Your monitor will display an error message at the first sign that something is terribly wrong with your computer. But what happens if your monitor is defective?

Problem:
Nothing appears on the monitor.

Solution:
1. Make sure the video adapter card is firmly plugged into the motherboard. Make sure that the cable is securely connected to the video adapter card to the monitor. Make sure the monitor is plugged in.

2. Adjust the contrast and brightness controls of you monitor. They may have been turned all the way down by mistake.

3. Check to see if the power on light is lit on your monitor. This indicates that the monitor is on and working, but isn't receiving any images. Replace the video adapter card.

4. If the power on light is not lit up on the monitor, you may have a dead monitor. Replace the monitor.

5. Your monitor may not work with your video adapter card. Some video adapter cards only work with certain types of monitor resolutions, like VGA, SuperVGA, etc. If your monitor and video adapter card are not compatible, they won't work. Replace either the video adapter card or the monitor.

Problem:
The images flicker or appear distorted.

Solution:
1. Check to see if other major electrical appliances may be plugged into the same electrical outlet as your computer and monitor, like a refrigerator, air conditioner, microwave oven, stereo, etc. Other items plugged into the same outlet may be sucking up electricity, causing temporary brownouts to your computer. Find an electrical outlet far away from any major appliance, and plug your computer in there.

2. Magnetic fields may be distorting your monitor's images. Move all speakers and other electrical items away from the monitor.

3. Adjust the controls on your monitor. They may have been knocked out of whack.

Keyboards and mice

Every computer needs a keyboard and most computers also need a mouse. If either of these items fails, then you're effectively locked out of your computer.

Problem:
The keyboard fails to work.

Solution:
1. Make sure the keyboard is securely plugged into the computer.
2. Look for a switch underneath or on the side of the keyboard. Some keyboards have a switch that lets them work with older XT computers or the newer AT computers. If the switch is set for the older XT computers, the keyboard won't work with the newer computers on the market. Set the switch to AT and reboot your computer.
3. Buy a can of compressed air and blow out the dust, hair, crumbs, etc. that may be cluttering the inside of your keyboard. For extremely filthy keyboards, unscrew the cover, take the keyboard apart, remove each key, and individually clean each contact with a blast of compressed air or a soft brush to remove any filth that may be preventing the keys from working properly. Use a cotton swab or Q-tip dipped in alcohol to clean the metal contacts of each key.
4. The keyboard may be dead. Replace it with a new one.

Problem:
The mouse cursor fails to appear.

Solution:
1. Make sure the mouse is connected properly to your computer's serial, bus, or PS/2 mouse port.
2. Most mice come with an installation program. Run the installation program again and make sure you correctly specify which serial port the mouse is connected to.
3. You may be missing the mouse driver programs MOUSE.COM and MOUSE.SYS. Microsoft Windows comes with these mouse driver programs, but MS-DOS does not. Buy a copy of Microsoft Windows or borrow these mouse driver programs from another computer.

Problem:
The mouse cursor moves erratically or sporadically.

Solution:
The mouse is likely sliding over a smooth surface or is gummed up with crumbs, dust, and other desktop debris. Buy a special mouse pad, and clean out your mouse by flipping the mouse upside-down and taking it apart.

Dealing with computer problems

If something is wrong with your computer and you have absolutely no idea what it might be, don't panic. Computers are strange electronic beasts with their own unique quirks. A computer that may work perfectly one day may suddenly shut down for no apparent reason the next day, and then work perfectly fine from that point on.

Any time you're completely stymied by a computer problem, don't be afraid to ask for help. Besides lugging your computer to the nearest repair shop, try leaving messages on local electronic bulletin board systems (BBSs) or on an on-line service like CompuServe or America OnLine. More than likely someone will have experienced the same or similar problem, and he or she will be able to offer you some clues on how to deal with it.

And don't forget about the dealer who sold you the part either. Most parts come with a standard one-year warranty, and dealers will be happy (and legally bound) to replace defective equipment. The dealers may even be able to help you with your problems, so give them a call. Many of the mail-order dealers provide special technical support hotlines just for this purpose.

Although myriad problems can go wrong with a computer, computers are actually fairly reliable beasts of burden. As long as you don't leave your computer exposed to the sun, freezing in an outside garage or patio, or smothered in an area that prevents air from circulating around it freely, and as long as you don't drop kick it or smack it with anything harder than your hand, your computer should work fine for years to come.

17
Software installation

Once you have installed your operating system, you're ready to start using your computer. The first step in preparing your computer is creating two files: the AUTOEXEC.BAT file and the CONFIG.SYS file.

The AUTOEXEC.BAT file is simply an ASCII file that contains a list of programs that you want your computer to run before doing anything else. The moment you turn on your computer, your computer immediately looks in the AUTOEXEC.BAT file for instructions on what to do next. Computers don't need an AUTOEXEC.BAT file, but it can be useful.

For example, many people run anti-virus programs to make sure their hard disk is free from viruses before doing anything else. Rather than type in the command to run your anti-virus program each time, you can let the AUTOEXEC.BAT file do it for you automatically.

The CONFIG.SYS file is another ASCII file that also loads programs for you every time you turn on your computer. But while the AUTOEXEC.BAT file can automatically load programs like word processors or Windows, the CONFIG.SYS file automatically loads programs necessary to make your computer work, like your mouse, scanner, CD-ROM drive, and sound card drivers.

Creating your AUTOEXEC.BAT and CONFIG.SYS files

When you install your sound card, mouse, scanner, or CD-ROM drive, you'll have to use a special installation program created by the manufacturer. These installation programs will usually create or modify your AUTOEXEC.BAT and CONFIG.SYS files for you.

If your computer doesn't have either an AUTOEXEC.BAT or CONFIG.SYS file, you can easily create one by typing EDIT (if you have MS-DOS or PC-DOS) or EDITOR (if you have Novell DOS). This command loads up a simple text editor which you can use to create your AUTOEXEC.BAT and CONFIG.SYS files.

A typical AUTOEXEC.BAT file might look like this:

```
set blaster=A220 D1 I5 T3
c:\sound\mscdex.exe /d:mvcd001 /m:10 /v
C:\DOS\SMARTDRV.EXE
PROMPT $p$g
PATH C:\DOS;C:\WIN;C:\SOUND;C:\UTILS
SET TEMP=C:\TEMP
\DOS\SHARE.EXE /L:500
```

The first two lines run programs to initialize the sound card and CD-ROM drive. The third line loads MS-DOS's SmartDrive disk caching program. The fourth line defines the DOS prompt to display directory names and a greater than sign like C:\DOS>. The fifth line defines the DOS paths. The sixth line defines a temporary directory called C:\TEMP. The seventh line loads the MS-DOS Share program.

Your sound card, CD-ROM drive, and Windows installation programs will probably (hopefully) create these lines in your AUTOEXEC.BAT file automatically, so it's not necessary to wonder about all the odd dashes, slashes, numbers, and letters scattered around. Just remember that your AUTOEXEC.BAT file gets your computer ready to work.

A typical CONFIG.SYS file might look like this:

```
DEVICE=c:\sound\mvsound.sys d:3 q:10 s:1,220,1,5 m:0 j:1 u
DEVICE=c:\sound\dd260.sys /d:mvcd001 /m:12 /p:340 /i:11
DEVICE=C:\CPCSCAN.SYS 3e0 2 1
FILES = 50
```

The first two lines initialize the sound card. The third line initializes the scanner. The fourth line defines how many files your computer can have open at any given time. Again, most of your computer scanner, mouse, sound card, or CD-ROM drive installation programs will create these lines in your CONFIG.SYS file automatically. One reason to edit your CONFIG.SYS file is to further optimize your computer for maximum performance. For example, MS-DOS 6.0 and greater includes a special power management program called POWER.EXE.

To use this program, you have to insert the following command in your computer's CONFIG.SYS file:

```
DEVICE = C:\DOS\POWER.EXE
```

The POWER.EXE program helps reduce the amount of power your computer needs when idle. Although this program is designed mostly to increase the battery power on laptop computers, you can use it on your desktop computer as well.

If your computer follows Microsoft's Advanced Power Management (APM) specification, expect your power savings to be up to 25% of its normal use. If your computer does not support the APM specification, your power savings may be up to 5%.

Once you have the POWER.EXE program running, you can check to see how much power it uses by typing the following at the DOS prompt:

```
POWER
```

Besides the MS-DOS power management program, you may want to invest in other utility programs that enhance your computer. Some of the common programs to increase the performance of your computer are:

- Disk doublers
- Memory managers
- Disk caches
- Backup program
- File recovery utilities
- Diagnostics programs
- Anti-virus

Disk doublers

Instead of buying a second hard disk, many people choose to buy a disk doubling program instead. A disk doubling program compresses the files on your hard disk so it can physically hold more files than normal. For example, a disk doubler program can convert a 120MB hard drive to hold approximately 200MB worth of files. Because disk doubling programs are so inexpensive and reliable, nearly everyone can benefit from a disk doubling program.

Of course, there's a price to pay with disk doubling programs. Some people have reported losing data when they first run a disk doubling program. Owners of older and slower computers may find that disk doubling programs slow their hard disk down to an intolerable level.

Because disk doubling programs have become so popular, nearly every operating system provides built-in disk doubling. MS-DOS uses a program called Double-Space, PC-DOS comes with a copy of a disk doubling program called SuperStor, and Novell DOS comes with a copy of Stacker.

Not all disk doubling programs are equal, though. Some compress files more tightly, leaving more free space on your hard disk. Others include utilities for recovering files damaged or lost during disk compression. As programs continue gobbling up more disk space, a disk doubling program belongs on every computer.

Stacker
Stac Electronics
5993 Avenida Encinas
Carlsbad, CA 92008
Tel: (800) 522-7822

Comments: Stacker is probably the most reliable and most efficient of all the disk doubling programs available. If you have already compressed your hard drive using MS-DOS's DoubleSpace program, Stac Electronics sells a version of Stacker that will convert your DoubleSpace hard drive into a Stacker hard drive. Because Stacker offers better file compression than DoubleSpace, converting to Stacker from Double-Space may give you a few extra megabytes of storage on your hard disk.

DoubleTools for DoubleSpace
AddStor, Inc.
1040 Marsh Road
Menlo Park, CA 94025
Tel: (415) 688-0470
Fax: (415) 688-0466

Comments: DoubleTools for DoubleSpace is designed to work with hard disks already compressed using MS-DOS's DoubleSpace program. DoubleTools provides maintenance tools to keep your DoubleSpace compressed hard disk working properly.

Memory managers

Every program you load uses memory. Unfortunately, you cannot avoid loading certain programs on your computer, like a software driver for your mouse, CD-ROM, scanner, or sound card. Most of these software drivers get loaded in a region known as conventional memory, which is the first 640K of your computer's total memory.

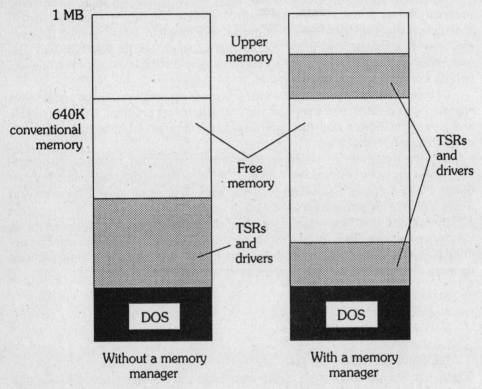

17-1 How a memory manager works.

To free up memory, memory managers move all software drivers out of conventional memory into a region known as high memory, which is the space between 640K and 1MB. Without a memory manager, your computer could have 32MB of RAM and yet give you an "Insufficient memory" error every time you try loading certain programs. With a memory manager, your computer can use its memory efficiently so you can run all the programs you want.

MS-DOS includes a memory manager called MemMaker, but if you want to squeeze the most memory out of your computer, then you'll need a separate memory manager program as well.

386Max

Qualitas Inc.
7101 Wisconsin Avenue, #1386
Bethesda, MD 20814
Tel: (301) 907-6700
Fax: (301) 907-0905

QEMM-386

Quarterdeck Office Systems, Inc.
150 Pico Blvd.
Santa Monica, CA 90405
Tel: (310) 392-9851

Comments: 386Max and QEMM-386 have been longtime contenders in the memory manager category. Both offer a nearly foolproof installation program that automatically configures your computer to use its memory most effectively, along with offering plenty of advice to help you modify your computer's CONFIG.SYS and AUTOEXEC.BAT files for maximum efficiency.

Netroom

Helix Software Company
47-09 30th Street
Long Island, NY 11101
Tel: (800) 451-0551
Fax: (718) 392-3100

Comments: Netroom was originally designed for network users, but has recently become popular among nonnetwork users as well. Besides managing memory, Netroom also includes a screen saver, disk cache, RAM disk, and antivirus utilities. For the most features for your money, Netroom currently is the leader.

Disk caches

A disk cache simply speeds up your computer. Many computers come with built-in disk caches, but a disk cache program can provide an additional boost in speed. Basically a disk cache guesses the most likely data the computer needs next off the hard disk and stores it in memory. When the computer needs the data, it reads it from the disk cache instead of from the hard disk. Because retrieving data from memory is much faster than retrieving data from a hard disk, your computer works faster.

MS-DOS comes with a built-in disk cache called SmartDrive, but for additional speed, you might want to use a separate disk cache program instead.

Cache86

The Aldridge Company
2500 Citywest Blvd., Suite 575
Houston, TX 77042
Tel: (713) 953-1940
Fax: (713) 953-0806

PC-Kwik
Multisoft
15100 SW Koll Parkway
Beaverton, OR 97006
Tel: (503) 644-5644
Fax: (503) 646-8267

Backup programs

With hard disks storing so many megabytes of data, it's important that you make backup copies in case your hard disk fails. To make backing up quick and easy, MS-DOS includes a backup program that automates the process.

Essentially a backup program compresses the files on your hard disk and stores them on multiple floppy disks or on a tape drive. You can selectively back up certain directories or certain files. Ideally you should back up your hard disk on a regular basis, like every month or every week. That way if your hard disk should crash, you will have a fairly recent copy of your files.

The Norton Backup

Symantec Corporation
10201 Torre Avenue
Cupertino, CA 95014
Tel: (800) 441-7234

Comments: The Norton Backup is available for DOS and Windows, as well as being sold as part of The Norton Desktop. MS-DOS's backup program is actually an older version of The Norton Backup. As a result, The Norton Backup is the only backup program that can restore files backed up using the MS-DOS backup program.

Central Point Backup

Central Point Software
15220 Northwest Greenbrier Parkway
Beaverton, OR 97006
Tel: (800) 445-4208

Comments: Central Point Backup is available for DOS and Windows, as well as being sold as part of PC Tools.

File recovery utilities

When you erase a file by mistake, the file still physically exists on the disk but your computer will ignore it. A file recovery program simply searches a floppy or hard disk for any files still on the disk, and it restores them so your computer can use them again.

Because file recovery can be so crucial, MS-DOS includes an Undelete program. The moment you erase a file, run the Undelete program to restore your file. The longer you wait to restore a file, the more likely your computer will overwrite it and destroy it when you save new data to the same disk.

The Norton Utilities
Symantec Corporation
10201 Torre Avenue
Cupertino, CA 95014
Tel: (800) 441-7234

Comments: The Norton Utilities is one of the oldest and most respected of all the file recovery programs available. A subset of The Norton Utilities can also be found in The Norton Desktop. Besides its ability to recover individual files, The Norton Utilities can also restore damaged disks.

PC Tools
Central Point Software
15220 Northwest Greenbrier Parkway
Beaverton, OR 97006
Tel: (800) 445-4208

Comments: PC Tools offers one of the most comprehensive utility packages for the price. In addition to file recovery capabilities, PC Tools includes a disk repair utility, an anti-virus program, a backup program, and a diagnostics program. MS-DOS 6.0 and higher even includes a subset of Central Point's Undelete program.

Diagnostic programs

A diagnostic program can tell you exactly what equipment your computer has, and whether it's working or not. Every new accessory you add to your computer requires certain equipment, like a serial port, IRQ address, or DMA channel. If your computer lacks the necessary equipment, your new accessory may not work with your computer. Even if your computer does possess the necessary equipment, the necessary equipment may not be working correctly.

MS-DOS comes with the Microsoft System Diagnostics program (MSD.EXE), which provides a quick summary of your computer's equipment. Both The Norton Utilities and PC Tools also come with a diagnostics program as well. However, if you want more detailed information, you need a separate diagnostics program instead.

CheckIt Pro: SysInfo
TouchStone Software Corporation
2130 Main Street, #250
Huntington Beach, CA 92648-2478
Tel: (714) 969-7746
Fax: (714) 960-1886

InfoSpotter Skylight
RenaSonce Group Inc.
Waring Road, #115
San Diego, CA 82120
Tel: (619) 287-3348
Fax: (619) 287-3554

Antivirus programs

Viruses are simply programs that duplicate themselves, spreading from computer to computer. Viruses are not necessarily dangerous or harmful, but they can be unwanted. At best, a virus will simply gobble up some disk space and display odd messages on your screen. At worse, a virus can wreck your hard disk, scramble your files, or make your computer act erratically.

To detect and remove a virus from your computer, you need a special antivirus program. MS-DOS comes with a subset of Central Point's anti-virus program while PC-DOS comes with IBM's own antivirus program.

Unfortunately, antivirus programs need constant updating as new viruses appear. Rather than rely on the antivirus programs provided with MS-DOS, many people choose separate antivirus programs instead.

Because new virus strains appear daily, the most effective anti-virus programs are often shareware versions that can be rapidly updated and distributed through on-line services and BBSs. Although no antivirus program is 100% effective, an antivirus program can protect you and your computer from most destructive viruses that could strike your computer.

F-Prot Professional
Command Software Systems
1061 Indiantown Road, #500
Jupiter, FL 33477
Tel: (407) 575-3200
Fax: (407) 575-3026

Comments: F-Prot Professional is also available on-line through CompuServe, GEnie, and local BBSs in a shareware version. While the shareware version lacks telephone support and a printed manual, it more than makes up for it with its $1 registration fee for private use. Among virus researchers around the world, F-Prot has established a reputation for being one of the most effective and accurate antivirus programs available.

ViruScan, VShield, Cleanup
McAfce Associates
3350 Scott Blvd., Bldg. 14
Santa Clara, CA 95054
Tel: (408) 988-3832
Fax: (408) 970-9727
BBS: (408) 988-4004

Comments: McAfee's collection of anti-virus programs are some of the most popular shareware programs available on-line. Because of its shareware distribution, McAfee's antivirus programs tend to get updated rapidly with each new generation of viruses.

18
Computer furniture

Owning an energy-saving computer built from recycled plastics may help save the environment, but it will do nothing to protect your own health. The first step to protecting your health is to get a keyboard and mouse that feels comfortable to you. The second step is to get the right furniture to position your keyboard, monitor, computer, and printer within easy reach and access.

Computer desks

When most people buy a computer for the first time, the computer inevitably winds up on any spare, flat surface like the kitchen table, the bed, or the living room floor. Naturally such ad hoc arrangements usually last until someone trips over the power cord or spills a sticky drink down the keyboard.

Because computers require so much room, most people buy a special computer desk. These computer desks usually have the following features:
- Shelves and cabinets to store books, floppy disks, and magazines
- A keyboard drawer so you can tuck the keyboard out of sight
- A monitor stand
- A flat surface for putting the computer on
- Another flat surface for the printer

The type of computer desk you buy depends on where you want to put it and what your computer looks like. For example, some computer desks are designed to fit snugly in the corner of a room, while others can be placed in a corner or along a wall.

Some computer desks have special shelves for mini-tower computer cases while others will work equally well with mini-tower or desktop cases. Make sure your computer desk also has plenty of room for other items besides your computer, like a telephone, notepad, or calendar. For some odd reason, most computer desks assume that once you have a computer, you'll never want any room left for taking notes, laying books open, or placing important papers nearby. If this describes your work habits, fine. Otherwise, make sure your computer desk has enough room for more than just a computer case and monitor.

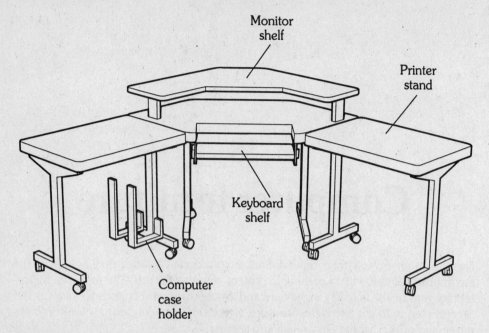

18-1 A typical computer desk.

Ideally a computer desk should hold the monitor approximately two feet from your eyes, in such a way that your neck isn't straining to see it properly. To eliminate eye strain from glare, make sure you have plenty of lighting, preferably overhead and directed downward away from your eyes.

Computer chairs

Because computer users tend to sit in one place for extended periods of time, the chair you use can affect your back, shoulders, and wrists. Ideally, a computer chair should have these adjustable features:

- Height
- Back support
- Arm rests

The height of the chair should allow your arms to reach the keyboard at a 90-degree angle and should allow your feet to rest flat on the floor. The back support should fit snugly into your back and keep it straight. Arm rests should prop up your elbows so your shoulder muscles don't have to hold up your elbows all the time.

For added comfort, a chair should have padding, tilt and swivel features, and casters so you can easily reach different areas of your computer desk without straining. A more unusual type of chair requires you to kneel in front of the computer, as if you're praying that the computer won't crash and destroy all your valuable work in a split second. Such a kneeling chair naturally forces your back to hold itself upright. However, these chairs rarely offer arm rests and can make your knees sore after using them for an extended period of time.

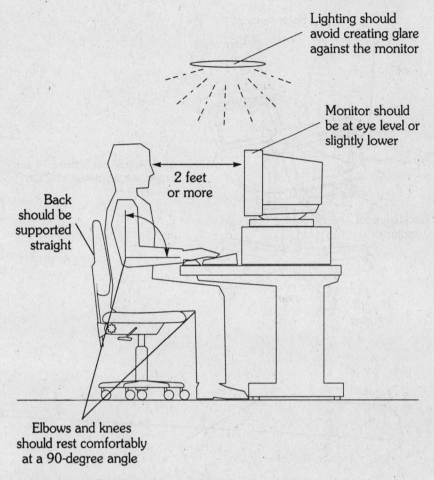

Lighting should
avoid creating glare
against the monitor

Monitor should
be at eye level or
slightly lower

2 feet
or more

Back
should be
supported
straight

Elbows and knees
should rest comfortably
at a 90-degree angle

18-2 Monitor and lighting recommendations for a computer desk.

Computer furniture buying cautions

Because computer furniture is relatively new, many furniture companies are building computer desks that look good but give no thought for actual use. For example, many computer desks offer keyboard drawers that let you tuck the keyboard safely out of sight.

Unfortunately, many of these keyboard drawers are self-enclosed containers, which means if you put the keyboard in the drawer, there's no place for the cord to connect to the computer. The only solution is to cut a hole yourself in the back of the drawer and hope your keyboard cord is long enough to reach the computer.

Another possible problem comes from printers. Some computer desks provide a flat surface for putting your printer, but no place to put any accompanying fanfold paper. The better computer desks provide slots at the top of the desk or in the back, where the feeding fanfold paper can be kept out of sight.

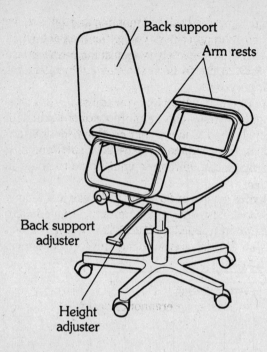

18-3 Adjustable features of an ergonomically designed chair.

Back support

Arm rests

Back support adjuster

Height adjuster

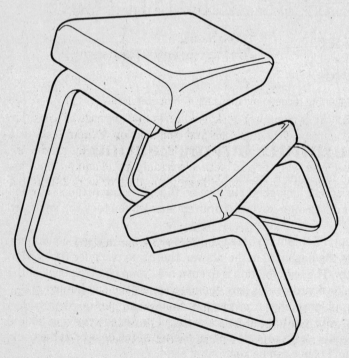

18-4 A kneeling chair.

If possible, measure the size of your computer case and monitor, and see if those measurements will fit comfortably on any computer desk you're thinking of buying. More than a few types of computer cases will completely swamp any available space on a computer desk, and some monitors refuse to fit in the tiny cubbyholes that some computer desks provide for that purpose.

Finally, many computer desks are modular, which lets you adjust the desk depending on what you need. Such modular desks can be more flexible because if you buy a new computer later on, or just need to move your computer desk to another room, you can adjust your desk to accommodate the new surroundings. Computer desks that remain in one shape can be more cumbersome to adapt in the future.

Ultimately, it doesn't matter what your computer furniture looks like just as long as you feel comfortable using it. The most expensive, ergonomically designed computer desk may pale next to a wooden door propped on four milk crates if you find this arrangement easier to use. The point is to adjust your computer for your convenience, and not the other way around.

Agio Designs
1400 NW Compton Drive
Beaverton, OR 97006-1992
Tel: (503) 690-1400
Fax: (503) 690-1444

Green Rating: *
(One star for ergonomic design)

Comments: This company sells a complete line of ergonomic computer desks and chairs. You can either order a predesigned computer desk from their catalog, or you can custom-design your own computer desk based on the parts they offer.

Anthro Technology Furniture
3221 NW Yeon Street
Portland, OR 97210
Tel: (800) 325-3841
Fax: (800) 325-0045

Green Rating: *
(One star for ergonomic design)

Comments: This company sells computer desks and carts that are easy to assembly and customize. To get a sample of the materials and construction of their desks, the company will sell you a special "Touch and Feel" kit. The cost of this kit can be applied towards a later purchase. They offer a lifetime warranty for all equipment, plus offer $50 off any purchase if you donate your old computer desk or workstation to a recognized charity.

BodyBilt Seating
3900 Texas Avenue
College Station, TX 77845-5831
Tel: (409) 693-7000

Green Rating: *
(One star for ergonomic design)

Comments: This company sells an ergonomic chair that can adjust in several different ways including seat tilt, backrest angle, seat height, backrest height, armrest height, armrest angle, and backrest depth. In addition to their chairs, BodyBilt also sells a program on CD-ROM that gives practical solutions for common seating problems.

Ergodyne   Green Rating: *
1410 Energy Park Drive   (One star for ergonomic design)
Suite One
Saint Paul, MN 55108
Tel: (612) 642-9889

Comments: This company sells a variety of ergonomic accessories to modify existing chairs for maximum comfort. Some of their products include wrist rests, foot rests, back supports that fit any type of chair, and Stretch Software, which displays twelve different types of stretches you can do while sitting in front of your computer.

Ergonomic Logic, Inc.   Green Rating: *
205 Vista Blvd., Suite 101   (One star for ergonomic design)
Sparks, NV 89434
Tel: (702) 331-6001

Comments: This company sells arm supports to relieve excessive stress in your back, shoulder, neck, arms, and wrists while using a computer. These arm rests can mount to any desk.

Grahl Industries, Inc.   Green Rating: *
One Grahl Drive   (One star for ergonomic design)
P.O. Box 345
Coldwater, MI 49036
Tel: (517) 279-8011
Fax: (800) GRAHL-07

Comments: This company sells ergonomic chairs with adjustable arm rests to support your elbows (especially good for people who constantly move their hands off the keyboard to use a mouse) and a unique two-piece back support that adjusts to the curvature of different people's bodies.

19

The future of green PCs

Not all green PCs are alike. The "lightest" green PCs just barely meet the Energy Star requirements to consume less than 30 watts of power when not in use. Although these "light" green PCs conserve electricity, they do little else to protect the environment. Because the U.S. government (the largest buyer of personal computers) has mandated that they will only buy Energy Star-compliant computer equipment from now on, every PC will soon be at least a "light" green PC. But as pollution becomes a growing problem and energy costs continue to rise, many computer manufacturers are taking the idea of a green PC one step further.

IBM sells two of the greenest computers on the market. In the North American market, IBM sells the IBM PS/2E. In the Asian market, IBM is test-marketing the IBM PS/55E. Both the PS/2E and PS/255E offers a 10-inch thin-film-transistor (TFT) color liquid crystal display, the same color display used in IBM's ThinkPad 750c notebook PC. Not only does this liquid crystal display require less power than a standard cathode-ray tube (CRT), but it takes up less space and doesn't emit any radiation.

Although physical space isn't much of a problem in America and, to a lesser extent, Europe, most people in Asian countries have much less space available to them. As a result, the physical size of a computer is a major factor for Asian computer buyers. Because many Asian companies sell computers in Asia and the rest of the world, you can expect the size of computers and equipment to start shrinking as well.

One major space-saving feature of the PS/55E is its combination keyboard and TrackPoint II pointing device. This type of keyboard eliminates the need for a separate mouse, reducing excessive hand movement from the keyboard to the mouse.

Instead of using bulky expansion cards, the IBM PS/55E uses PCMCIA cards, which take up less space, require less material to make, and consume less power. Even better, such PCMCIA cards can be easily swapped between computers quickly and easily.

One of the biggest problems with the Energy Star program is that the Energy Star guidelines don't specify the maximum amount of power a computer can consume while in use. Ordinary Energy Star compliant computers can consume up to 100 watts of power when in use. In comparison, the PS/2E and PS/55E consume less

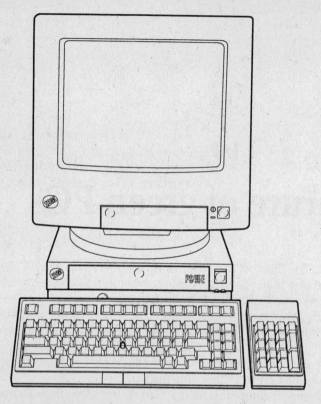

19-1 The IBM PS/55E.

than 50 watts of power while in use and drop down to 12 watts when not in use. For a truly green PC, a computer needs to conserve power all the time, not just when the user walks away from it.

Best of all, IBM built the PS/2E and PS/55E using recycled plastics that can be snapped apart for easy assembly and disassembly. When you finally have to throw out your computer, you can save all the plastic parts for recycling.

Judging from the IBM PS/2E and PS/55E, the green PCs of tomorrow will borrow heavily from the laptop technology of today. As green PCs become the norm, expect to see the following changes in future computers:

- Built from recycled plastics
- Built-in serial, parallel, game, and SCSI ports
- Built-in floppy/hard drive controller
- Low power consumption while in use and even more reduced power consumption when not in use
- Small size and light weight
- Use of PCMCIA expansion cards instead of standard expansion cards and slots
- Integrated keyboard/pointing device to reduce space requirements and excessive hand movement
- Color liquid crystal displays that don't emit any electromagnetic radiation
- Ability to run off batteries
- Uses "dark green" chips

Because circuit boards and electronics require toxic chemicals to manufacture, there will always be a risk to the environment from toxic wastes, and a risk to human health from workers exposed to these chemicals. To avoid these problems, many manufacturers are working on a "dark green" chip, also dubbed an "all-vegetable" chip. Such a "vegetable" chip will eliminate the use of toxic chemicals altogether and may use chemical reactions similar to photosynthesis, hence the nickname of a "vegetable" chip.

The green PC you build today will likely appear clunky and wasteful next to the green PCs of tomorrow. Yet every little step helps, and if you switch to a green PC now, you'll be making your contribution to saving the environment and you'll be saving money in electricity costs as well. Given that incentive, can anybody afford not to use a green PC of their own?

A
APPENDIX

Converting an existing PC into a "green" PC

To convert an existing PC into a "green" PC, you have to modify your current computer in three ways:

- Reduce your computer's electricity requirements to meet the Energy Star guidelines.
- Reduce your monitor's electromagnetic radiation emissions.
- Reduce your printer's use of electricity, paper, ribbons, cartridges, and other consumables.

"Green" power strips

The simplest way to reduce your computer's energy requirements is to plug your computer, monitor, keyboard, and printer into a special "green" power strip.

These "green" power strips consist of the power strip itself plus a special program that lets you define the amount of time you want the power strip to wait before reducing the electricity to your computer or monitor. When the "green" power strips senses that no one has touched the keyboard after a certain amount of time, it reduces power to any items plugged into the "green" power strip, like your computer, monitor, and printer.

To reactivate your computer and monitor, just tap the keyboard and the power strip brings the monitor and computer back to life. Because these "green" power strips are completely separate from the computer, these "green" power strips can work with any type of computer or monitor.

Like many types of ordinary power strips, "green" power strips may or may not include surge suppression. Basically a surge suppressor protects your computer equipment from drastic electricity surges or spikes, which can damage electronics. Because a surge suppressor can protect your computer, it's a good idea to buy a "green" power strip that includes built-in surge suppression.

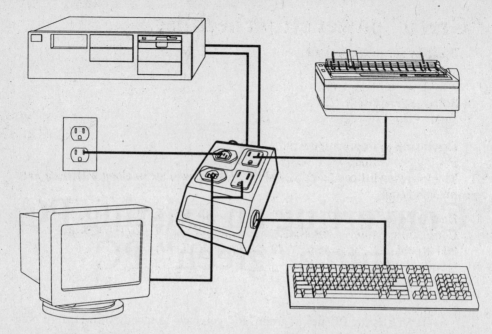

A-1 A typical "green" power strip with the computer, monitor, keyboard, and printer plugged in.

Certain "green" power strips have other flaws as well. Because these "green" power strips require you to load a special program before they can work, you'll lose a certain amount of RAM that won't be available for running your other programs.

Even worse, these special programs that activate the "green" power strip may only work for certain operating systems, like MS-DOS, Windows, or OS/2. When shopping for a "green" PC, make sure its software will work with your operating system.

Heavy mouse users may dislike "green" power strips for another reason. Because "green" power strips work only by monitoring keyboard activity, they won't reactivate your computer or monitor if you move the mouse; you have to tap the keyboard instead.

If you use a mouse extensively, you may find the "green" power strip shutting down your computer and monitor in the middle of your work. While you won't lose any data during this shutdown period, it can be annoying to have your monitor blank out periodically while you're using it.

Shopping for a "green" power strip

Not all "green" power strips are equal. The following checklist shows the various features to look for in a "green" power strip.

"Green" power strip checklist

Built-in surge suppressor:
Yes   No

Software required:
Yes   No

Operating systems supported:
MS-DOS   Windows   OS/2

The following list compares available "green" power strips along with their various pros and cons.

Energy Saver
Contek International Corporation
303 Strawberry Hill Avenue
Norwalk, CT 06851
Tel: (203) 853-4313
Fax: (203) 853-6414

Green Rating: *
(One star for meeting the Energy Star guidelines.)

Built-in Surge Suppressor: Yes
Software Required: Yes
Operating Systems Supported: MS-DOS and Windows

Green Keeper
B&B Electronics
4000 Baker Road
P.O. Box 1040
Ottawa, IL 61350
Tel: (815) 434-0846
Fax: (815) 434-7094

Green Rating: ***
(One star for meeting Energy Star guidelines.)
(One star for using 100% recycled packaging and recycled floppy disks.)
(One star for donating $1 from every purchase to the Global ReLeaf reforestation project.)

Built-in Surge Suppresser: No
Software Required: Yes
Operating Systems Supported: MS-DOS, Windows, and OS/2
Comments: The Green Keeper only reduces power to your monitor, printer, or other external peripherals. It will not reduce power to the computer itself.

Monitor Saver
Cypress Computer, Inc.
Eden Landing Road
Suite 6
Hayward, CA 94545
Tel: (510) 786-9106
Fax: (510) 786-9553

Green Rating: *
(One star for meeting Energy Star 26120 guidelines.)

Built-in Surge Suppressor: No
Software Required: No
Operating Systems Supported: MS-DOS, Windows, and OS/2

Comments: The Monitor Saver only powers down your monitor, not your computer
or printer.

PC Ener-G Saver
PC Green Technologies
Centerpointe Drive
#210
La Palma, CA 90623
Tel: (714) 228-2230
Fax: (714) 228-2239

Green Rating: *
(One star for meeting Energy Star
  guidelines.)

Built-in Surge Suppressor: Yes
Software Required: Yes
Operating Systems Supported: MS-DOS and Windows

Power Miser
Tripp Lite
500 N. Orleans
Chicago, IL 60610-4188
Tel: (312) 329-1777

Green Rating: *
(One star for meeting Energy Star
  guidelines.)

Fax: (312) 644-6505

Built-in Surge Suppressor: Yes
Software Required: No
Operating Systems Supported: All
Comments: The Power Miser uses a physical switch to adjust the time-out period.
This lets the Power Miser work with any type of operating system or computer.

"Green" add-in card

As another alternative to plugging an existing computer into a "green" power
strip, some companies are now offering "green" expansion cards that plug into your
computer's expansion slot. Such a "green" card can reduce electricity to the computer and monitor (if the monitor's plugged into the computer and not into a separate power outlet), meeting the requirements of the Energy Star program.

For more information about "green" add-in cards, contact:

Progen Technology, Inc.
3115 Airway Avenue
Costa Mesa, CA 92626
Tel: (714) 549-5818

Green Rating: *
(One star for energy-saving features)

Mecer Corporation
29560 Union City Blvd.
Union City, CA 94587
Tel: (510) 476-5730
Fax: (510) 475-0982

Green Rating: *
(One star for energy conserving features)

Micro Express
1801 Carnegie Avenue
Santa Ana, CA 92705
Tel: (714) 852-1400

Green Rating: *
(One star for energy-saving features)

Monitor shields

Besides reducing your computer and monitor's energy requirements, you also need to reduce your monitor's electromagnetic emissions. Because you can't see, smell, or otherwise sense electromagnetic radiation, it's difficult to know how much your monitor may be emitting. To detect emission levels that exceed the MPR II Swedish standard for safety, consider buying a radiation meter. By placing the radiation meter next to your monitor, you can see and hear where radiation levels may be too high.

Because the strength of radiation decreases with distance, the safest and simplest solution is to sit further back from your monitor. Another common solution is to use a radiation filter that shields you from any electromagnetic radiation.

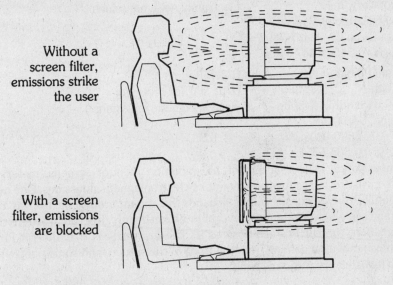

Without a screen filter, emissions strike the user

With a screen filter, emissions are blocked

A-2 A typical screen filter.

The following list describes available products you can buy that claim to reduce electromagnetic emissions from your monitor. Prices vary depending on the size of the screen filter you need for your particular monitor.

Axelen Glass Filter AGF-14
Axelen, Inc.
15621 S.E. 11th Street
Bellevue, WA 98008-5009
Tel: (206) 643-2781
Fax: (206) 643-4478

Green Rating: *
(One star for reducing electromagnetic emissions.)

Ergo-Cover
Ergo-Vision Plus2
Spectrum Universal
Glare Screen

Green Rating: *
(One star for reducing electromagnetic emissions.)

Kantek, Inc.
15 Main Street
East Rockway, NY 11518
Tel: (516) 593-3212
Fax: (516) 593-3295

Comments: The Ergo-Cover drapes over the sides and back of most monitors, where the highest level of radiation occurs. Because the Ergo-Cover doesn't cover the front of the monitor, you will need to use the Ergo-Cover along with a screen filter as well. The Ergo-Vision Plus2 fits over the front of most monitors, blocking most forms of radiation.

Glare/Guard
Optical Coating
Laboratory, Inc.
2789 Northpoint Parkway
Santa Rosa, CA 95407-7397
Tel: (800) 545-6254

Green Rating: *
(One star for reducing
electromagnetic emissions.)

NoRad Shield
NoRad
1160 E. Sandhill Avenue
Carson, CA 90746
Tel: (310) 605-0808
Fax: (310) 605-5051

Green Rating: *
(One star for reducing
electromagnetic emissions.)

Comments: NoRad sells a variety of anti-radiation monitor screens, meters, and shields to measure and reduce any monitor's electromagnetic emissions. One device, called the Elf Protech, consists of metal bands that mount around the back and sides of your monitor, where the highest level of radiation occurs. Instead of attempting to block radiation, the Elf Protech absorbs it. The drawback is that the Elf Protech doesn't block radiation coming from the front of the screen, and some people might object to its ugly appearance as well.

Rad Alert
RAD Devices, Inc.
3231 Union S.E.
Grand Rapids, MI 49548
Tel: (616) 452-7750
Fax: (616) 452-5560

Green Rating: *
(One star for measuring
electromagnetic emissions.)

Comments: The Rad Alert device attaches to a monitor and continually measures its radiation level. The moment the radiation exceeds the MPR II standard for acceptable radiation, it sounds an audio warning and displays a red light.

Vu-Tek Anti-Glare Filters
Optical Devices, Inc.
805 Via Alondra
Camarillo, CA 93012
Tel: (805) 987-8801
Fax: (805) 388-1123

Green Rating: *
(One star for reducing
electromagnetic emissions.)

Wristsaver
Eye Protection Filters
LB Innovators, Inc.
2524 Main Street
Suite H
Chula Vista, CA 91911-4670
Tel: (619) 745-2383
Fax: (619) 423-1060

Green Rating: *
(One star for reducing
 electromagnetic emissions.)

Converting a printer to a "green" printer

Connecting a printer to a "green" power strip can cut its electricity requirements, but you can reduce your printer's consumable items like ribbons, cartridges, and paper as well. Because every printer uses paper, the easiest choice is to buy only recycled paper.

According to the Environmental Protection Agency, paper that is marketed as "recycled paper" must contain a minimum of 50% paper waste. Of course, paper waste can be either preconsumer or postconsumer waste.

Preconsumer waste contains paper remnants and materials that were discarded before ever being sold. Postconsumer waste consists of paper collected from businesses and individuals after it has already been used. When comparing recycled paper, look for paper made mostly out of postconsumer waste.

Recycled paper typically lists the percentage of recycled fibers used plus the percentage of postconsumer waste used. For example, recycled paper might claim 50% recycled and 10% postconsumer waste. This means 50% of the paper fibers are virgin fibers and 50% consists of recycled fibers. Out of those 50% recycled fibers, only 10% came from postconsumer waste while the other 40% came from preconsumer waste. Ideally, the "greenest" paper consists of 100% postconsumer waste.

The following lists paper suppliers who sell recycled paper for laser printers and copiers.

Atlantic Recycled Paper Company
P.O. Box 39179
Baltimore, MD 21212
Tel: (800) 323-2811
Fax: (410) 323-2681
Comments: Besides selling recycled paper for laser printers and copier machines, the Atlantic Recycled Paper Company also sells recycled envelopes, fax paper, tissue, stationery, towels, facial tissues, paper cups, and business card stock.

Paper Direct
205 Chubb Avenue
Lyndhurst, NJ 07071-0618
Tel: (201) 507-1996
Fax: (201) 507-0817

TreeFree Eco Paper
121 S.W. Salmon, Suite 100
Portland, OR 97204
Tel: (503) 295-6705
Fax: (503) 690-4051

Comments: TreeFree Eco Paper sells laser printer and copier machine paper made from 50% hemp and 50% cereal straw, bleached with hydrogen peroxide, making this paper the most environmentally safe on the market. The paper is naturally acid-free, giving it a shelf life of 1500 years, compared to traditional wood-based paper that must be treated with zinc oxide to neutralize the acid that breaks down the wood fiber. Such acid-free, hemp paper is made using the same process first discovered by a Chinese monk in the year 75 AD. For the most environmentally friendly paper around, this is your only choice.

Ribbons and cartridges

Besides paper, the next most crucial item for printers includes ribbons (for dot-matrix printers), ink cartridges (for inkjet printers), and toner cartridges (for laser printers). Once a ribbon or cartridge has been used up, don't toss it out. Recycle it.

Ribbons can be reinked or reloaded, ink cartridges can be refilled, and toner cartridges can be remanufactured. The cost of reusing a ribbon or cartridge can be up to half the amount of buying a brand new ribbon or cartridge.

Reinking a ribbon means keeping the original fabric ribbon inside the ribbon cartridge and adding fresh ink to it. Ribbons can only be reinked a certain number of times before the ribbon gets too worn out.

Reloading a ribbon cartridge means yanking out the old fabric ribbon and replacing it with a new, fresh ribbon. Because you're using a new ribbon each time, there's no theoretical limit to the number of times you can reload a ribbon cartridge.

Refilling an ink cartridge means squirting fresh ink back into an empty ink cartridge. Remanufactured toner cartridges have been disassembled, cleaned, inspected, refilled, and tested to meet or exceed your printer manufacturer's specifications.

The following lists companies that sell reloaded ribbon cartridges, refilled ink cartridges, and remanufactured toner cartridges.

Advantage Laser Products, Inc.
2030 Powers Ferry Road, Suite 218
Atlanta, GA 30339
Tel: (404) 953-2515
Fax: (404) 953-6993

Comments: Advantage Laser Products sells remanufactured toner cartridges for laser printers. Such remanufactured toner cartridges are used cartridges that have been disassembled, inspected, cleaned, and refilled.

Image Control Corporation
200 Pearl Street, Suite 200
Buffalo, NY 14202
Tel: (716) 842-6015
Fax: (716) 842-6049

Comments: Rather than dump your used inkjet cartridges, Image Control will sell you ink refill kits. By using their refill kits, you can refill your used inkjet cartridges at much less cost than buying new inkjet cartridges. The whole process of refilling an inkjet is fairly simple and quick.

Quality Recharge Company
3965 Park Avenue
St. Louis, MO 63110
Tel: (314) 865-0929

Comments: This company accepts your used laser toner cartridges and in return, they'll test, disassemble, clean, lubricate, refill, and ship the cartridge back to you.

Repeat-O-Type Manufacturing Corporation
665 State Highway 23
Wayne, NJ 07470
Tel: (201) 696-3330
Fax: (201) 694-7287

Comments: Repeat-O-Type sells inkjet cartridge refills and laser printer toner so you can refill your own toner cartridges. The company claims that refilling your used cartridges can reduce solid waste up to 92%.

The Ribbon Factory
2300 E. Patrick Lane, #23
Las Vegas, NV 89119
Tel: (702) 736-2484
Fax: (702) 736-1054

Comments: The Ribbon Factory accepts your used ribbon cartridges and reloads them with a fresh ink ribbon.

Floppy disks

Even though every computer has a hard disk, everyone still has to use floppy disks once in a while. Rather than buy a fresh box of floppy disks each time, consider buying recycled floppy disks instead.

Recycled floppy disks come from outdated software packages. Rather than dump outdated software in landfills, software publishers sell them to companies that specialize in recycling all the manuals, boxes, shrink-wrap, and floppy disks. After erasing the floppy disks, relabeling them, and verifying that they are virus-free, these companies sell these used floppy disks back to the general public. Because these used floppy disks have never been used at all, they'll work just as well as a new floppy disk.

For more information about buying recycled floppy disks, contact one of the following companies:

Convenant Recycling Services
P.O. Box 2530
Del Mar, CA 92014
Tel: (619) 792-6975
Fax: (619) 792-1599

GreenDisk
15530 Woodinville-Redmond Road
Suite 400
Woodinville, WA 98072
Tel: (206) 489-2550

Softdisk Publishing
606 Common Street
Freeport, LA 71101
Tel: (318) 221-8718
Fax: (318) 221-8870

B
APPENDIX

Recycle your old computer

Although you can upgrade your current computer to meet the Energy Star guidelines, you may decide it's more convenient to buy a brand new one instead. Rather than toss out your old computer or abandon it in a closet or garage, donate it to a charity. That way your computer will still be used and you'll get to take off a tax deduction besides.

Any charity will gladly accept a used computer, from public libraries and churches to the Red Cross and the American Cancer Foundation. Even if you don't have a charity in mind, or if your old computer needs repairs, then you can donate your computer to one of the following special organizations.

These organizations specialize in refurbishing and repairing used computers and placing them where they're needed the most. To donate your used computer equipment, contact one of the following organizations:

CompuMentor
89 Stellman Street
San Francisco, CA 94107
Tel: (415) 512-7784

Comments: This organization accepts new, complete, unused software (the latest versions) to sell to various nonprofit groups for a minimal price. Some of the recipients of CompuMentor's program have been the Red Cross, the Montana Wilderness Association, and Friends of Oakland Park and Recreation. Besides software, CompuMentor will also accept computers (286 and up or Macintosh SE and up) that are complete and in working condition.

Computer Recycling Center
1245 Terra Bella
Mountain View, CA 94043
Tel: (415) 428-3700

Comments: This organization distributes donated equipment to California schools and provides ongoing support for hardware and software. In addition, they also train individuals in computer maintenance.

Computers and You
330 Ellis Street
San Francisco, CA 94102
Tel: (415) 922-7593
Fax: (415) 922-0756

Comments: This organization provides a computer education and training center for disadvantaged children, low-income families, the homeless, and drug and alcohol recoverers. Their mission is to provide access to computers for people who don't normally have access.

Detwiler Foundation Inc. Computer for Schools Program
470 Nautilus Street, Suite 300
La Jolla, CA 92037
Tel: (619) 456-9045
Fax: (619) 456-9918

Comments: Accepts donations of computer hardware and software to place in California schools. The Detwiler Foundation will also accept broken or damaged equipment, which will be used to train students in vocational computer repair classes. Besides donating computer hardware and software, you can also donate office furniture, cabinets, telephones, copy machines, fax machines, and other office-related equipment.

East-West Education Development Foundation
49 Temple Place
Boston, MA 02111
Tel: (617) 542-1234
Fax: (617) 542-3333

Comments: The East-West Education Development Foundation refurbishes computer equipment and donates it to American charities that perform life support human services, and overseas charities that focus on education, democracy, free market economies, and human rights. Some of the charities that receive computers from the East-West Education Development Foundation include the Epilepsy Foundation, Cape Cod Hospital, the African Wildlife Foundation, Human Rights in China, and the Institute of Peace and International Security.

National Cristina Foundation
591 West Putnam Avenue
Greenwich, CT 06830
(800) 274-7846

Comments: The National Cristina Foundation focuses on teaching and training disabled and disadvantaged children. Some of the charities that receive computers from the National Cristina Foundation include the United Cerebral Palsy Association, the Easter Seal Society, the Council for Exceptional Children, and the North Carolina Division of Vocational Rehabilitation.

Non-Profit Computing Inc.
2124 Wall Street
New York, NY 10005-1301
(212) 759-2368

Comments: Distributes donations of computers and other telecommunications equipment and software to various nonprofit groups. For more information about donating equipment, send them a self-addressed, stamped envelope.

C
APPENDIX

"Green" books, magazines, and organizations

Once you finish building your own "green" PC, don't stop there. Learn more and get involved with other people who share your interests. The more you learn about environmental issues, the better the decisions you can make for yourself.

Books

Carpal Tunnel Syndrome: Prevention & Treatment
by Kate Montgomery
Sports Touch Publishing
P.O. Box 229002-155
San Diego, CA 92122
Comments: Carpal tunnel syndrome is fast becoming the most prevalent problem affecting people who use a computer extensively during the day. To prevent carpal tunnel syndrome, this book provides plenty of stretching exercises that anyone can practice while sitting at their keyboard.

Currents of Death: Power Lines, Computer Terminals, and the Attempt to Cover Up Their Threat to Your Health
by Paul Brodeur
Simon and Schuster
1230 Avenue of the Americas
Comments: This was the first (and most shocking) book to publicize the dangers of electromagnetic emissions from common technology that most people take for granted, like power lines, television sets, and computer monitors. If you want to learn more about the problems and the attempts of various organizations to dismiss the dangers of electromagnetic emissions to your health, this is the book to read.

EcoLinking
by Don Rittner
Peachpit Press
2414 Sixth Street
Berkeley, CA 94710

Comments: Finding other people interested in the "green" PC movement isn't always easy. If you have a modem, this book will help you find ecology-minded organizations and individuals from various on-line services like CompuServe, America Online, GEnie, Prodigy, and the Internet. In addition, the book contains information about lesser-known computer networks like EcoNet, which is part of a worldwide network operated by the Institute for Global Communications and the Association for Progressive Communications. EcoNet can link you to people and environmental groups around the world, including some in Brazil, Russia, Sweden, and Uruguay.

The Green PC: Making Choices that Make a Difference
by Steven Anzovin
Windcrest/McGraw-Hill
Blue Ridge Summit, PA 17294-0850

Comments: An introductory book that explains the growing "green" PC movement, the hidden health hazards of computer equipment, and techniques for reducing your computer's impact on the environment. Each chapter comes loaded with manufacturers' addresses and phone numbers to help you find the environmental resources that you need to make your computer a little bit "greener."

How to Survive Your Computer Workstation
by Julia Lacey
CRT Services
Workstation Consultants
P.O. Box 420127
Laredo, TX 78042

Comments: Headaches, eyestrain, and fatigue are all symptoms of staring at a computer monitor for too long. To avoid or relieve these problems, this book contains simple exercises and solutions that people can do to protect themselves from their computer monitors.

In the Absence of the Sacred: The Failure of Technology & the Survival of the Indian Nations
by Jerry Mander
Sierra Club Books
730 Polk Street
San Francisco, CA 94109

Comments: Think technology is always good? Think again. In this book, the author makes convincing arguments that technology should examined with a more skeptical eye because all technology has inherent drawbacks that everyone should know about. Besides listing seven negative points about computers that you'll never find discussed in computer magazines, the author describes how society's fascination and blatant approval of technology is threatening our own survival as a society, as well as demolishing the societies of indigenous people around the world.

NIOSH Publications on Video Display Terminals
National Institute for Occupational Safety and Health
Division of Standards Development and Technology Transfer
4676 Columbia Parkway
Cincinnati, OH 45226
Comments: This book contains various studies concerning video display terminal (VDT) use and its effect on humans. Some of the report titles contain in this book are *VDTs and the Risk of Spontaneous Abortion, A Review of VDT Studies and Recommendations*, and *Controlling Glare Problems in the VDT Work Environment.*

Magazines

E: The Environmental Magazine
28 Knight Street
Norfolk, CT 06851
Tel: (203) 854-5559

Earth Island Journal
300 Broadway
San Francisco, CA 94133
Tel: (415) 788-3666

Green Alternatives for Health and the Environment
38 Montgomery Street
Rhinebeck, NY 12572
Tel: (914) 876-6525

Greenpeace
1436 U Street, NW
Washington, DC 20009
Tel: (202) 462-1177

Sierra
Sierra Club
Polk Street
San Francisco, CA 94109
Tel: (415) 776-2211

Organizations

CAREIRS (Conservation and Renewable Energy Inquiry and Referral Service)
P.O. Box 3048
Merrifield, VA 22116
Tel: (800) 523-2929
Comments: CAREIRS provides information on all types of renewable energy technologies, energy conservation, and recycling. Besides supplying brochures, books, and fact sheets, CAREIRS also can refer you to various trade associations, federal agencies, and professional groups involved with energy conservation.

Global ReLeaf
P.O. 2000
Washington D.C. 20013
Tel: (800) 8-ReLeaf

Comments: Global ReLeaf is the national and international action and education campaign of American Forests. The goal is to improve the environment by planting and caring for trees. Many computer companies are Global ReLeaf sponsors, like the mail-order giant Gateway Computers.

Greenpeace
1436 U Street, NW
Washington D.C. 20009
Tel: (202) 462-1177

and

Greenpeace
4649 Sunnyvale Avenue, North
Seattle, WA 98103
Tel: (206) 632-4326

Comments: Greenpeace is one of the more active and visible of the environmental organizations that often provokes the ire of many companies and even foreign governments. The organization gladly welcomes any volunteer assistance you may care to give. Contact the Greenpeace organization nearest you, or call the Greenpeace bulletin board system (BBS) at (415) 861-6503.

Interesting software

Federal SoapBox
SoapBox Software
10 Golden Gate Drive
San Rafael, CA 94901
Tel: (415) 258-0292
Fax: (415) 258-0294

Comments: The "green" PC movement and related environmental activities can be initiated at an individual level, but eventually you may need to reach people in various government agencies. Rather than do all the research yourself to find the phone numbers, people, and agencies to contact, get the Federal SoapBox program instead. This program contains a complete database of all the people in cabinet level departments, public service agencies, committees and subcommittees of Congress, and the Federal Court system. Every three months the company will send you an updated database. Not only will this program help you locate the people who can make the changes you want, but it will also help you write your letters and send them through MCI Mail.

Vision Aerobics
Vision Aerobics, Inc.
10 Mechanic Street, Suite G
Red Bank, NJ 07701
Tel: (908) 219-1916
Fax: (908) 219-9697

Comments: If you suffer from eyestrain while using a computer, load Vision Aerobics on your computer and let this program provide various eye exercises to strengthen your vision. According to independent studies conducted by an exercise psychologist at the University of Maryland, daily use of Vision Aerobics for 10 minutes a day, over a three-week period resulted in increased ability to make rapid eye movements, form coordinated images, and change focus from near to far objects. With regular eye exercise, you can delay or eliminate eye fatigue from staring at your computer monitor for long periods of time.

Glossary

Adapter A piece of equipment that helps connect two items together, such as a cable to a port.

Add-on An accessory program or computer part that enhances or improves the existing equipment.

AMD Acronym that stands for American Micro Devices, which is a company that specializes in making microprocessors for IBM compatible computers.

AMI Acronym that stands for American Megatrends International, which is a company that specializes in making BIOS chips for IBM compatible computers.

Antivirus A program that catches and removes computer viruses from floppy and hard disks.

APM An acronym that stands for Advanced Power Management, which is a specification designed by Microsoft to conserve power.

ASCII An acronym that stands for American Standard Code for Information Interchange. ASCII defines a universal code for representing information so all types of computers can exchange information with one another.

AUTOEXEC.BAT A file that stands for <BCU> autoexec<ECU> utable <BCU> bat<ECU> ch file. This file contains a list of all programs to run before the computer gives the user an opportunity to use the computer.

Backlit To illuminate a screen from behind to make it easier to read. Often used in laptop computer screens.

Baud A unit that measures the speed a modem of fax board transfers information. Common baud rates are 2400, 9600, 14400, and 28800. Often used interchangeably with bps.

BBS Acronym that stands for Electronic Bulletin Board System, which are public or private computers used for exchanging files and messages with other people.

BIOS Acronym that stands for Basic Input/Output System. The BIOS chip determines how a computer works.

bps Acronym that stands for Bits Per Second, which measures the speed that a modem or fax board transfers information. Often used interchangeably with Baud.

Buffer Special memory designated for temporarily storing information.

Bus mouse A type of mouse that plugs into a special expansion board.

Cache Special memory that speeds up a computer by guessing which data the computer needs next.

Carcinogen A substance known to cause cancer.

Carpal tunnel syndrome A physical condition that affects the nerves in the wrists. Often occurs through repetitive, unnatural motion of the hands and arms, such as using a keyboard for long periods of time.

Centronics port Another name for a parallel or printer port.

CFCs Acronym that stands for ChloroFluroCarbons, which is a cleaning solvent for circuit boards known to deplete the ozone.

CMOS Acronym that stands for Complementary Metal-Oxide Semiconductor, which is a specially designed circuit used to store a computer's floppy and hard drive settings.

Cold boot To turn on a computer after it has been turned off.

CONFIG.SYS An acronym that stands for CONFIGuration File, which loads device drivers for the computer to use, such as mouse, sound card, CD-ROM, and scanner drivers.

Conventional memory The first 640 kilobytes of your computer's memory.

Co-processor A secondary processor designed specifically for performing mathematical calculations.

cps Acronym that stands for Characters Per Second, which is a way to measure the speed of printers.

CPU Acronym that stands for Central Processing Unit, which is the main chip that performs all calculations.

DD Acronym that stands for Double-Density, which is used to describe the storage capacities of floppy disks. DD type floppy disks are slowly fading from use.

Device driver A special program that tells your computer how to use certain attached equipment such as a mouse, a scanner, and a CD-ROM drive.

DOS An acronym that stands for Disk Operating System, which is a special program used to control IBM compatible computers. The three most popular versions of DOS include MS-DOS (from Microsoft), PC-DOS (from IBM), and Novell DOS (from Novell).

DoubleSpace A program included with MS-DOS 6.0 and higher to compress files on a hard disk and effectively increase the amount of files the hard disk can store.

dpi Acronym that stands for Dots Per Inch, which describes the sharpness of print resolution from inkjet and laser printers.

DPMS Acronym that stands for Display Power Management Signaling, which is a standard for reducing power to monitors.

DRAM Acronym that stands for Dynamic Random Access Memory. An inexpensive and slower type of memory chip that requires constant updating from the computer. DRAM chips are often used in place of more expensive VRAM or SRAM chips.

ED Acronym that stands for Extended-Density, which is used to describe the storage capacities of floppy disks. ED type floppy disks are 3.5 inches in size and can hold up to 2.88 megabytes of data.

EISA Acronym that stands for Extended Industry Standard Architecture, which is an enhanced design of the original ISA bus design.

ELF Acronym that stands for Extremely Low-Frequency, which are electromagnetic emissions that come from electronic equipment.

Energy Star The logo created by the Environmental Protection Agency to designate computer equipment that complies with defines levels of power usage when idle.

EPA Acronym that stands for the Environmental Protection Agency.

Ergonomics The science of designing equipment for maximum human comfort and efficiency.

Expansion card A circuit board designed to plug into a computer, enhancing or improving the computer's capabilities.

Expansion slot An opening in a motherboard that lets you plug in additional circuit boards to enhance the capabilities of your computer.

FAX Acronym that stands for Facsimile, which is a way of transferring information as graphic images through the phone lines.

FCC Acronym that stands for Federal Communications Commission. The FCC tests equipment for their electrical shielding abilities. An FCC Class B rating means that equipment can be safely used in a home or office. An FCC Class A rating means that equipment can only be safely used in an office. To verify any system's FCC Class rating, dial the FCC's own bulletin board system at (301) 725-1072.

Floptical A type of floppy disk capable of storing twenty megabytes per disk. Floptical disks require the use of a special floptical disk drive.

Footprint The physical size of an item, describing how much room it requires on a flat surface.

Game port A special plug used to connect a joystick to your computer.

GB Acronym that stands for Gigabyte, which is a measurement of storage capacity and represents a billion bytes.

HD Acronym that stands for High-Density, which is used to describe the storage capacities of floppy disks. Sometimes this acronym is also used to represent a Hard Disk in computer advertisements.

IDE Acronym that stands for Integrated Drive Electronics, which is a standard for controlling hard disks.

Interface The connection between two items, such as a cable and a port.

Internet A worldwide computer network that links universities, companies, and individuals together through modems.

ISA Acronym that stands for Industry Standard Architecture, which is the design of the original IBM PC back in 1981.

Joystick A pointing device often used by games.

LAN Acronym that stands for Local Area Network.

LCD Acronym that stands for Liquid Crystal Display, a flat screen display most often found on laptop computers.

LED Acronym that stands for Light-Emitting Diode, which is a device that lights up when an electrical current passes through it.

LQ Acronym that stands for Letter Quality, used to describe the print resolution of dot-matrix printers.

MB Acronym that stands for Megabyte, which is a measurement of storage capacity and represents a million bytes.

MCA Acronym that stands for Micro Channel Architecture, which is an alternate bus designed by IBM for the original PS/2 computers. Rarely used today.

Memmaker A memory management program included with MS-DOS 5.0 and higher to optimize your computer's memory for maximum efficiency.

MIDI Acronym that stands for Musical Instrument Digital Interface, which is a standard for encoding music in digital form.

Mini-Tower case A computer case that stands upright and can fit under or on top of a desk.

Motherboard The main circuit board in a computer that contains the processor, memory, and expansion slots.

Mouse A pointing device that looks like a small bar of soap.

MPC Acronym that stands for Multimedia Personal Computer.

MPR II A Swedish standard that defines how much electromagnetic emissions a monitor can release and still be within acceptable safety levels.

MTBF Acronym that stands for Mean Time Between Failure, often used to give a rough estimate on how long a piece of equipment will continue working.

Multifunction An adjective that describes any computer part that offers one or more features.

NLQ Acronym that stands for Near Letter Quality, which describes the print resolution of dot-matrix printers.

OS/2 An alternate operating system from IBM, designed to provide multitasking along with a graphical user interface.

PCI Acronym that stands for Peripheral Component Interconnect, which is a new bus design for computers.

Pentium An advanced microprocessor developed by Intel, which is the next generation up from the 80486 family of processors.

POST Acronym that stands for Power-On Self-Test, which is what every computer goes through to see if everything works okay each time you turn the computer on.

Postconsumer waste Waste products that are recycled from material sold to consumers.

Preconsumer waste Waste products that were discarded during manufacturing, and were never sold to consumers.

PostScript A page description language used to create fancy effects for printing, often used for desktop publishing.

PowerPC An advanced microprocessor developed by Motorola. The latest generation of Apple Macintosh computers use this processor as well as some IBM computers.

ppm Acronym that stands for Pages Per Minute, which is a measurement of printing speed for laser printers.

RAM Acronym that stands for Random Access Memory, which is the memory used by computers to run programs.

Recyclable Means that the material is capable of being recycled and reused over again, but may be made out of virgin materials. Not to be confused with Recycled.

Recycled Means that the material has been made from previously used materials. Not to be confused with Recyclable.

Resolution The appearance of multiple dots, used to display information on paper or on a monitor screen.

RF Acronym that stands for Radio-Frequency.

RFI Acronym that stands for Radio-Frequency Interference.

RS-232 Another name for a serial port.

RSI Acronym that stands for Repetitive Strain Injury.

Scandisk A utility program included with MS-DOS 6.2 that inspects floppy and hard disks for errors and fixes them when they occur.

SCSI Acronym that stands for Small Computer System Interface, which is a standard for connecting computer accessories together.

Shareware Software that you can legally copy and give away, but if you continue using it, you're supposed to pay for it.

SIMM Acronym that stands for Single In-line Memory Module, which are memory chips.

SIPP Acronym that stands for Single In-Line Pin Package, which are memory chips that are fast being replaced by SIMM memory chips for common use.

Slimline case A computer case that sacrifices expansion capabilities in exchange for its small size.

SMM Acronym that stands for System Management Mode, which is a specification for conserving power in a computer.

SRAM Acronym that stands for Static Random Access Memory. An expensive but fast type of memory chip. SRAM chips a are often used in place of DRAM chips for extra speed.

Surge suppressor A device that prevents massive changes in electrical voltage from damaging computer equipment.

Tower case A computer case that looks like a column and is almost as high as a normal desk. Tower cases are often used when maximum expansion capabilities are needed, such as for a network server.

Trackball An alternate pointing device that uses a stationary ball to move a cursor on a screen.

TSR Acronym that stands for Terminate and Stay-Resident, which is a special type of program that loads itself in memory and remains there even when other programs are loaded and running.

UPS Acronym that stands for Uninterruptable Power Supply, which is a device that maintains power to your computer in the event of a power outage.

VESA Acronym that stands for the Video Electronics Standards Association, which is an organization that defines standards for video displays.

Virus A program capable of self-replication. Viruses are often destructive and unwanted.

VL-bus Acronym that stands VESA Local bus, which is a special bus designed for working with video adapter cards to speed up graphics.

VRAM Acronym that stands for Video Random Access Memory. A type of memory chip used in place of DRAM chips for video adapter cards. VRAM chips are faster and more expensive than DRAM chips.

Warm boot To restart a computer without turning it off.

Windows A program made by Microsoft that makes computers easier to use by providing a graphical user interface, letting users run programs by clicking the mouse on icons and choosing commands from pull-down menus.

ZIF Acronym that stands for Zero Insertion Force, which is a special socket that lets users easily remove and install a central processing unit to their motherboard.

Index

Shareware disk offer

Besides the utility programs that come included with MS-DOS, PC-DOS, or Novell DOS, you may want additional utility programs to enhance or improve your computer's performance. You can find a multitude of such utility programs available commercially and through shareware sources like BBSs, on-line services like CompuServe, or local computer user groups.

But if you'd rather not hunt around for useful shareware utility programs on your own, just send $10 to the address listed and you'll receive the following programs:

Burn-In

Once you finish building or buying a new computer, you have to burn it in by leaving it on for two days to two weeks straight. If anything is going to fail in your computer, the chances are high that it will fail during such a burn-in period.

Leaving your computer turned on will certainly test your computer, but to give your computer a more rigorous workout, you can use this special Burn-In program instead. This program exhaustively tests every part of your computer from your hard drive to your monitor.

If anything fails, the Burn-In program will provide a report to let you know what went wrong.

CMOS_RAM

Every computer includes a built-in battery to keep track of the date, time, memory, and the number and types of your machine's drives. You'll have to run your computer's SETUP program when you use your computer for the first time, and you'll have to run the SETUP program again any time you add or remove any equipment.

But what happens if this built-in battery fails? It's inevitable, and when the battery does fail, your computer will lose all of its configuration data needed to work. Then you'll have to buy a new battery and re-enter your computer's CMOS data all over again.

Instead of writing down all of your CMOS settings and storing them in a safe place somewhere, just run the CMOS_RAM program, which stores all of your CMOS settings on a floppy disk. Then when your built-in computer battery fails, just run the

CMOS_RAM program off your floppy disk and it will quickly restore all of your CMOS settings.

F-Prot

At last estimate, there were over 2,500 viruses loose in the computer world. While most of these viruses are harmless, a few can be destructive to the point of erasing your hard disk data. Although MS-DOS and PC-DOS come with a built-in antivirus program, don't rely on them.

According to an independent study that tested various antivirus programs against a collection of 2,000 different viruses, the MS-DOS antivirus only caught 48% of the viruses, which meant that 52% of the viruses slipped by and infected the computer.

Even worse, many virus programs are specifically designed to avoid or neutralize the MS-DOS antivirus program. For maximum safety, you should use an independent antivirus program instead. One of the best antivirus programs is called F-Prot.

In the same test against 2,000 viruses where the MS-DOS antivirus only caught 48% of the viruses, F-Prot caught 95%, scoring the highest of all antivirus programs on a list that included The Norton antivirus, IBM's antivirus, and Central Point's antivirus programs.

Developed in Iceland, F-Prot is one of the few antivirus programs equally effective against viruses developed in America, Europe, and Asia. This program is updated regularly, and if you send away for the shareware disk offer, you'll be assured of getting the latest version.

Meg

The Meg program displays a pie graph, showing the amount of storage space available on any floppy or hard disk, the amount of storage space currently being used, and the amount of storage space still available. By using this program, you can quickly check the amount of free space available on any computer's hard disk.

Sleep

Most computers use hard disks that follow the IDE standard. Unknown to most people, however, IDE hard disks have the ability to "spin down" when not in use, conserving power. While this feature is most often used in laptop computers, it's also available for desktop computers as well.

To activate this energy-saving feature of your IDE hard drive, just run the Sleep program and specify how many minutes of inactivity you want the computer to wait before "spinning down" the hard drive. The Sleep program doesn't require any memory, nor does it affect the performance of your hard disk in any way. By using this program, you can further help ensure that your computer will be as "green" as possible.

In addition to these shareware programs, you'll also receive a game (to make sure your computer works properly, of course), the phone number to my own private BBS where you can download additional utility programs, plus the latest utility programs that may appear after publication of this book. Feel free to photocopy the following form and use it to order.

Please send disk requests to:

Wallace Wang
Box 348, Palm Avenue
Chula Vista, CA 91911

I have enclosed $10 to cover shipping and handling.

Choose the type of the floppy disks you want the programs stored on:
5.25-inch high-density (1.2MB)   3.5-inch high-density (1.44MB)
5.25-inch double-density (360K)   3.5-inch double-density (720K)

Name: _____

Address: _____

City: _____ State: _____ Zip: _____